Naked Truths, Imagination &

BIG
IDEAS

Create the Next Blockbuster
for Your Business

PHOTO: MARQUEZ WHITEHEAD

Paul Rienzo is an expert in identifying innovation opportunities, developing new products and marketplace communication. With over thirty years at Procter and Gamble, he has broad experience across more than twenty categories in a range of roles from upstream R&D to downstream commercialization, from introducing new to the world products to reviving established brands. He has been recognized for excellence in leading multifunctional teams to breakthrough results.

Acknowledgments

Thanks to Shellie Porter Caudill and Jason Merrill Jones for their help in unwinding Big Ideas.

TABLE OF CONTENTS

- Workshop Designs
- Beachcombing Verbs
- Naked Truth Templates

1: INTRODUCTION

What is a Big Idea?

"We need more Big Ideas!" is a familiar call to action. But few can tell you what one is. When pressed, most will describe it in terms of what it *does:*

> "Makes a lot of money."
> "Creates buzz."
> "Something we can own."
> "People remember it."
> "Changes the game."
> "Killer ad campaign."

It's all true, but none are a definition of Big Idea. The term originated in architecture:

> A **Parti** or **Parti pris** / from the French **Prendre parti** meaning " to make a decision ", often referred to as **the Big Idea**, is the chief

organizing thought or decision behind an architect's design presented in the form of a basic diagram and / or a simple statement.

- Wikipedia

An Architect designs an important building with Big Idea in mind. It inspires creativity and helps to make choices, right down to the smallest construction details.

If you've been asked for a Big Idea, then you've been charged with finding a compelling, central organizing thought that will drive and shape all aspects of the proposition's design and communication.

There is demand for Big Ideas because they 1) focus development programs on what matters and ultimately proprietary breakthroughs, and 2) rise above the communication clutter in the marketplace, attracting consumers to what they offer. They change the game and reset the rules. And they have staying power.

The First Big Idea

Big Ideas are found throughout human history. Many could lay claim to the being the first one in consumer goods. But let's look at Ivory Soap, which had a couple of blockbusters in the 1890s.

Procter & Gamble introduced Ivory in 1879. Ivory was different from other bars because it was whipped with air, making it less dense than water. "It floats" first appeared in print in 1891. For many years, magazine and poster ads pictured people bathing with a bar bobbing in plain view. Bathers found it frustrating to fish for soap at the bottom of the tub in cloudy water. Floating soap solved the problem.

"99 $\frac{44}{100}$% Pure" was an even more successful Big Idea for the brand. It was supported by "Eastern University" studies that determined its analytical purity. The ingredients in soap were well known to consumers, since it was not unusual for homemakers (or their grandmothers) to make their own soap. Tallow soap is made with animal fat and lye. Unreacted lye is harsh on skin and this was understood as the main impurity, which is what made the claim meaningful. Ivory was purer than its chief competition, castile soap.

It is remarkable that both Big Ideas outlived their relevance. Ask someone what comes to mind with "Ivory Soap" and they are likely to say at least one of the phrases. But few would be able to give a reason that either statement would matter. Most Americans shower today and the majority don't wash with a bar. So, they can't imagine the benefits of a floating bar.

"99 $\frac{44}{100}$% Pure" is an iconic term that has become part of the American Lexicon. It is sometimes paraphrased in other contexts. Award winning John Frankenhiemer directed a movie called "99 $\frac{44}{100}$% Dead". Few know that the original phrase refers to the absence of a caustic material. Mild synthetic cleansers largely replaced tallow soap many years ago.

Recognizing a Big Idea

"I know it when I see it" is often said about Big Ideas.   But it would be better to have a little more clarity if it's your job to come up with one. They share these traits:

- **Simple**
  It is expressed with a picture or a few words.

- **Explains itself**
  It is descriptive without ambiguity. It makes sense.

- **Contractual**
  It is a contract between the company and consumers, making a promise to purchasers while setting goals for development.   A Big Idea isn't a Big Idea if it can't be delivered.

- **Meaningful**
  It connects to an important consumer need, a Naked Truth.

- **Reframes**
  It introduces a new frame of reference so the product or service is no longer seen in quite the same way. It elevates the importance of it, or an aspect of it… often in a surprising way.

- **Unforgettable**
  It captures attention and sticks in the head.

- **Inspirational**

It's easy to imagine how it will influence all aspects of invention and execution.

Types of Big Ideas

There is more than one kind of Big Idea. The five types are discussed in detail in Chapter 4, but here is a brief overview:

- **Evidence**

  It is a moment in which the advantages of the product or service are most evident and relevant.

- **Providence**

  It has credentials, certifications or approvals that matter to consumers.

- **Specialization**

  It is an innovation that has been created to address greater needs of special people, conditions or tasks.

- **Transformation**

  It describes results or change with a metaphor or analogy that has meaning and value to people.

- **Mimic**

  The innovation manifests itself as an intuitive, appealing metaphor or analogy.

About this Book

The aim of this book is to make finding a Big Idea certain; to make a pipeline of Big Ideas inevitable. It gives you powerful thinking frameworks and tools to generate Big Ideas for any business. It's as relevant to the work of independent entrepreneurs as it is to large multifunctional teams. It promises to transform your development process.

You will still brainstorm, but take better aim. You will still do qualitative research, but go deeper and more directly. You will still have to do all the things you would do to develop your innovation and communication, but making better decisions and choices along the way.

There are four phases in producing a Big Idea: Discover, Connect, Imagine and Realize. This book outlines your itinerary, explains theory in plain talk, provides illustrative examples and covers the nuts and bolts of research and ideation.

Avoid Common Traps

Before launching into the content, it may be helpful to cover four common traps with Big Idea generation:

- **Jumping In**
  It's tempting to start brainstorming before doing homework on the consumer, the marketplace or solutions that already

exist. The team that jumps in produces output that is familiar and uninspiring; a recycling of flawed and limited ideas from past efforts. So, take time to discover what motivates your consumer, drives your market, and limits the satisfaction with today's solutions. Time can be a pressure to take a short cut. But remember that there is never seems to be enough time to do it right, but there always seems to be enough time to do it over.

- **Concept Instead of Big Idea Development**
  Less than fifty years ago, the written concept revolutionized advertising and product development. Studies proved that consumers' reaction to written descriptions of an idea was predictive of success in the marketplace. However, concept development is often misused to find a Big Idea, rather than to describe one. Or worse, has been solely focused on achieving a high score without regard to clarity for marketing or R&D. It's common for "winning" concept to lack a clear Big Idea.

- **Linear Brainstorming**
  Big Ideas connect across three domains: the consumer, the marketplace and the innovation itself. Each is a huge frontier to understand, so it's not surprising that many ideate on these domains independently, or on only one of them. Consumer-led ideation works on the question, "What do they need?" It usually produces a long list of ideas, few of which are actionable. Market-led ideation asks,

"What's working?" The output tends to be a list of me-too ideas. Product-led ideation focuses on, "Why would they want it?" Those ideas generally turn out to be unappealing or niche.

- **Marketing Only**

  Big Ideas should influence all aspects of innovation. They drive awareness and trial when leveraged in marketing. But focusing exclusively on communication without regard to performance is a recipe for a fad. Some consumers may try it, but will be disappointed if the experience doesn't deliver the promise. Imagine an electric car that claims to be "The first electric with as much horsepower as a diesel engine." You think, "Wow, that's what I've been waiting for." So, you go to the nearest dealer for a test drive. But you can't hit the highway speed limit when you floor it. The car looks styled for a family of four instead of having a high-performance design. You're disappointed. You're definitely not going to buy that car, and may never waste your time to test drive another one from that maker. You may tell your friends so they aren't disappointed as well.

Case Study – Part 1

This case study will unfold at the end of each chapter. It is fictional story, imaginary and hypothetical. It includes pretend, yet plausible qualitative and quantitative findings and information. Its only purpose is to illustrate a typical journey to a Big Idea if this guide is followed.

Big Food is a conglomerate which produces many different food products. Their goods can be found in nearly every aisle of grocery stores. Big Food has just made a major acquisition and Acme, a small candy brand, was part of the deal. It's not clear how the little candy maker fits since the CEO is refocusing the entire organization on healthy snacks and meals. That's why management is already discussing divestiture.

Jack works for Big Food and his boss has given him a new assignment, to come up with a Big Idea for the Acme brand. "It's gone if you don't," he said.

Jack meets with some of the employees who work at the Acme Candy Factory. They are a committed group who are worried about their jobs. Jack asked to speak to someone from Research and Development, but was told they don't have an R&D Department. It's because Acme makes old fashioned packaged candy from traditional recipes like Swedish fish, gummy bears, rock candy and lollipops. It's the kind of stuff found at Cracker Barrel restaurants, old time country stores and movie concession stands. They also make holiday novelties, like molded chocolate bunnies for Easter, popcorn balls for Christmas and candy corn for Halloween.

Jack's trip left him discouraged about finding a Big Idea for Acme, yet he was impressed with the factory's quality control and candy making know-how. He believed that Acme had the equipment and expertise to make anything.

2: DISCOVER

John Wooden won ten national championships at UCLA over a 12-year period. His teams captured 7 titles in a row. No other team has more than two in a row. They also won a record 88 consecutive games in that span. Wooden was named national coach of the year six times. His greatness was not evident in the 28 years of coaching that preceded his first national title. He explained…

> "It's what you learn after you know it all that counts."

> -   **John Wooden**

Discovery is more than accumulating data and facts, their source must also be found… the deep, undercurrent truths that shape reality. It's the same for someone exploring unfamiliar territory as it is for anyone re-examining an area of personal expertise. Undercurrent truths should be the objective. They are "drivers" or "factors" in statistical analysis. Qualitative researchers name them "insights." Scientists may declare them "laws" or "theories". Marketers may say "trends."

A deeper truth usually hides behind other truths that have spawned from it. So, to find it, you must strip away lesser or irrelevant facts. It can also be obscured by flawed, prevailing models. Sometimes a different point of view is necessary to see it. Since it doesn't become obvious until exposed by analysis, call it a **Naked Truth**.

Nicolaus Copernicus published a heliocentric theory of the solar system in 1543. It departed from the Ptolemaic theory in which the planets and sun revolved around the Earth. Astronomers had worked with the Ptolemaic model for centuries. However, "fudge factors" and "work arounds" were necessary to fit the model to observed motions in the heavens. Numerous empirical equations were implemented.

Copernicus was troubled by the complexity and exceptions in the accepted theory and the empirical system surrounding it. He looked for an alternative construct and found that putting the sun at the center made the math work better. His model was perfected in the generations that followed him, but his book is often regarded as the start of modern astronomy and the Scientific Revolution. The Earth revolving around the sun is a Naked Truth in physics.

Repeated, unexplained observations are clues for Naked Truths. They may be cast aside since they are beyond the scope of exploration or unrelated to the stated problem being solved. Some oppose common wisdom so they are dismissed. They can be simply ignored since there is nothing to address them, even if they are a "500-pound gorilla in the room". Here are a few qualitative consumer research anecdotes about Naked Truths:

A new researcher interviewed a young mother about fabric softener. Mary told him about the scents she liked, that she preferred liquid softener to dryer sheets, her preferred brand and why. The conversation could have ended there since she'd answered all the questions on the research guide. But there were two things made the researcher curious.

She had said on her recruiting questionnaire that she had used liquid softener in the past month, but she was currently using dryer sheets. So, he asked Mary when she had last used liquid softener. She said that it had been about two weeks. Her washer had broken and she didn't have the money to fix it, so she was going to the laundromat.

Several times she remarked that she liked using fabric softener because it was something nice she could do for her baby girl. The researcher asked her to tell him about her baby girl. Chloe was born with a hole in her heart and had to have surgery. But Mary was a single mom without health insurance and couldn't afford the operation. She was putting off major purchases in the hope that should could someday, which was why she hadn't replaced her washer.

Making her daughter's clothes soft and smell good was a way "of doing something nice for her." That was crucial to her since Mary didn't know how long her baby girl would be with her. She was willing to buy fabric softener, but it was too heavy to take with her to the laundromat. The single use pouches available at the place were pricy, and she couldn't justify paying for convenience. So, Mary had switched to dryer sheets when her washer broke since they added next to no weight to her basket. It didn't leave the clothes soft like a liquid, so she was still actively looking for a practical way to bring softener to the laundromat. She was thinking of pouring some softener in Tupperware, but hadn't taken that step yet.

Fabric softener cares for her baby girl's clothes, so using it is an expression of her love. But its bulky packaging makes dryer sheets a better option, even though they don't leave the clothes as soft.

Another researcher explored wrinkle removal from clothes for a different project. She interviewed many women about dealing with wrinkles and what would interest them as an alternative method or device for ironing.

Jane was one consumer who spent many hours ironing, often late at night when everyone had gone to bed. She sometimes stopped her kids from walking out the front door with wrinkled clothes, making them undress so she could iron. Making her family look good was important to her and she was willing to put in the effort, even though she really didn't like ironing.

But it didn't add up for the researcher... especially the iron that Jane brought with her as part of the interview. The white plastic covering had yellowed with age and the aluminum heat plate was dull and mottled with corrosion. It looked like an economy model that could be picked up Walmart for less than ten bucks. She unsuccessfully probed what Jane wanted in a new iron. Finally,', she asked, "there are professional models that seamstresses own; have you ever considered one of those?" Jane replied, "Why would I spend money on something I hate to do?"

She spends many hours ironing because she wants her family to look good when they walk out the door. Although there are premium irons that would do a better job, she won't spend money on something she hates to do.

A project team had generated a quantitative segmentation model for hair care. They conducted focus groups to better understand the segments. One segment was of particular interest since they frequently had "bad hair days" and didn't know how to get the look they wanted. These consumers seemed like they could be ripe for innovation because their dissatisfaction was higher than any other segment.

There was a striking difference in their appearance compared to the other segment focus groups conducted previously. The other women had been well dressed, wore make-up and had styled their hair. These women wore sweat pants, no make-up, and had pony tails sticking out of their baseball caps.

The warm-up exercise used in all groups was, "if you were a shoe, what kind would you be?" Women had said that they would be a pair of "stiletto heels", "Jimmy Choos", or Birkenstock sandals. But this segment gave odd answers. Amy said she would be a pair of Keds. Tommi grinned that she would be a cleat.

Like the other women in the room, Karen claimed to be having a bad hair day. She said she was frustrated with her hair, but unexplainably hadn't attempted to style it that morning. She dressed for the group like she did every day, and it apparently did not bother her to wear disheveled clothes in public. She only wore make-up on special occasions, like weddings. She disliked shopping the beauty aisle and did not enjoy getting her hair done at the salon.

The team mined the quantitative study and discovered that Karen's segment spent the least amount of time and money on their beauty routine. These women didn't enjoy beauty care and had largely opted out of the category. But our culture pressures women to look their best. The team concluded that stating, "I'm having a bad hair day" excused their behavior in social settings, so they wouldn't be judged negatively by their peers.

> *Some women don't put much into their beauty routines because they don't enjoy it and would rather invest time and money in other things. But they fear being judged negatively, so they may say that they are having a bad hair day to excuse her appearance.*

Naked Truths distill knowledge into digestible nuggets that minds can wrap around easily. They stand by themselves and do not require further explanation, although they can be bolstered with data and examples if they exist. This chapter introduces a few indispensable tools and thinking constructs that will reveal critical "Naked Truths" about your consumer, market and product.

Three-Letter Words

"Why", "but" and "how" are key to revealing Naked Truths and grounding imagination in reality. Asking "why" strips away shallow and irrelevant information to get to the underlying currents that shape the innovation space. Identifying "but" finds discontent, dissatisfaction and issues that lead to opportunities for innovation. Asking "how" transforms vague notions into realistic solutions and actions. These three-letter words should be the mindset of innovators.

Human Needs

Chance Meeting

"How are you?"

"Pretty good!" *(Except my knees have gotten so bad that I have to give up running.)*

"How's your beautiful wife?"

"Busy, busy, busy!" *(Trying to find meaning in her life after the youngest went off to college last year.)*

"Any plans for the summer?"

"Not really, it's been crazy, so we just want to take it easy this year." *(Because we've got three others in college and can't afford it.)* *"How about you, are you doing anything fun?"*

****

There are deep human needs that aren't shared with strangers, and sometimes not even with family. But they can play in your head whenever the right subject triggers it. Sometimes they live in back of your mind where even you may not be aware of them, not realizing that they are influencing your behaviors and choices.

These needs have different names, including unmet consumer, client or customer needs and insights. Unearthing a deep human need is the discovery of one type of Naked Truth. Big Ideas are anchored in broadly shared Naked Truths about deep human needs. In this book, they will be referred to as "consumer needs" or "Need Naked Truths" or just "Needs".

While people may keep some Naked Truths private, they all arise from a finite set of shared human needs. They motivate us to buy products, experiences and services to fulfill them. Many can be described as functional problems, others as emotional stress. They are connected, for functional problems cause emotional stress. For example, someone who says that they don't have enough *time* (functional) can feel *overloaded, trapped or inadequate* (emotional) as a result. Lists of 24 functional problems and 11 emotional stresses follow.

Functional Problems

Barrier	Dissonance	Unknown
Risk	Gap	Inescapable Truth
Difference	Paradox	Conflict
Compromise	Incapability	Return on Investment
Imbalance	Complexity	Support
Compensate	Loss	Disorder
Control	Time	Consequences
Interruption	Effort	Unpredictable

Emotional Stress

Frustration	Disappointment	Guilt
Inadequacy	Overloaded	Loneliness
Trapped	Cheated	Wanting More
Unappreciated	Fear	

Universal Problems

The first step in consumer understanding is to discover which of these functional problems and emotional stresses are driving choices and behavior. The list below is written in more accessible language:

Not worth the time or money
Can't ignore it
Has a short coming
I have compromised
It takes more than I can do
It's chaotic or messy
Different from what I want
I don't know how
I feel cheated
In conflict
It's thankless
There is discomfort
There is a barrier
I don't have time
The risk is high
I am afraid of...
If feel trapped

I feel frustrated

I feel inadequate

Not addressing the real problem

Has an undesirable consequence

It's too complex

I've given up, accepted

It doesn't work together

It's out of balance

Can't have it both ways

I don't have the resources

Out of Control

Less than ideal

I crave more

There is a gap

I feel guilty

I feel unique, alone

I feel disappointed

Darned if I do, Darned if I don't

I'm overloaded and overwhelmed

It causes interruption/gets in the way

I've lost what I had at one time

I have to compensate in other ways

I have settled for something less

It's unpredictable

Problem Cards

Put these statements on flash cards for qualitative consumer research. For one-on-one research, give them to your interviewees and ask them to pick out the three cards that are most relevant to the topic being discussed. Then ask why they picked the ones that they did.

It's also terrific stimulus to kick off a focus group. Have participants work in pairs to select the most relevant one for them, then ask them to introduce one another with the selected cards. This works well as a warm-up for three reasons, 1) people easily relate to the cards, so they prompt animated discussions, 2) participants make a friend when they work in a pair, and that puts them at ease in the group discussions that follow, and 3) it elicits unbiased learning on the topic from the start, instead of chewing up valuable time on an unrelated "fun" exercise.

Try the cards with your team too. Deal out cards and ask them to jot down how each problem is relevant to your consumer, based on what they know about them. Have them write directly on the card. Pass them around until the cards are filled. Debrief the group on what they believe was most critical to the project. This silent ideation method is preferable to group brainstorming for this task; thoughts can flow so quickly that it's impossible to keep up with charting, even with multiple scribes.

Use them to incite your personal thinking. Turn the list into a worksheet and capture what you know. If you can't find at least one example for each statement, you may want to do more investigating.

Choice Research

I went out for breakfast the other day. I thumbed through the restaurant's eight-page morning menu and the laminated breakfast special insert. There were manager's specials written on the chalk board mounted over the counter. I didn't feel like having anything fancy that morning, so I decided to get their most popular plate.

"What can I get you?" The waitress said as she whipped out her check pad.

"I'll have the 'Rise and Shine'."

"How do you want your eggs?"

"Fried."

"Over easy?"

"Can you flip them? I don't like them runny."

"Toast, pancakes, muffin or biscuits?"

"Toast."

"White, whole wheat or rye?"

"Whole wheat, no butter, please."

"Jam for your toast?"

"Yes, please."

"We have grape, blackberry, strawberry, and apple butter."

"Sugar free?"

"Yes, we have sugar-free grape. Hash browns or home fries?"

"Home fries."

"Sausage or Bacon?"

"Sausage."

"Patties or links?"

"Links."

"Would you like juice with that? We have orange, cranberry, and apple."

"No thanks, I've got coffee." Thankfully she had already poured me a cup when I sat down. Too many decisions to make on an empty stomach.

"Would you like a refill?"

"Yes, could you make the next one decaf?" I replied.

"Of course."

"You wouldn't happen to have any flavored creamer, would you?"

****

A Cornell University study (Wansink, Sobal: 2007) found that the average person makes over 200 food choices every day. But some of these choices are not choices at all. I replied "links" as thoughtlessly as I would have rattled off my phone number. I relied on a prior decision and previous experiences. My day will be full of choices and I want to spend my brain power on what really matters. So, when it came to breakfast, I got to go with what I know, at least on this day. Because I'm shopping at Walmart after breakfast and a typical store stocks about 100,000 different products.

Discovering how choices are made is another key to consumer understanding. It requires more than simply tracking what they buy, you must know why they prefer links over patties. Further, you should know what will nudge consumers to reevaluate their settled choices.

Constant Sum Research

Constant sum is a powerful research tool to understand how consumers think. People are given points to divide across features and benefits to customize for their needs. A basic example of the method follows, try it out!

****

A leading automobile manufacturer wants to learn how it can make better cars. Thinking about how you would improve your CURRENT vehicle, please place the 10 stars (stickers) that you have been given on the sheet below. Divide the stars between the characteristics to create what would be best for you.

How Would You Improve your Current Vehicle?	
Better Gas Mileage	
More safe to drive	
Lasts longer	
Less frequent maintenance	
Better Sound System	
More storage space	
Better for environment	
More passenger space	

****

If you tried it, then you probably experienced a high level of involvement with the task. It gets you thinking, which is why it yields so much insight about consumers.

When you've made a board for your own space, sit with volunteers while they do the exercise and ask them to "think out loud". If you listen for their reasoning it won't be long before you'll be able to think like them. This simple constant sum approach can be conducted in quantitative research too. But it must be coupled with enough qualitative interviews to understand the true meaning of the data.

Constant Sum Game

Elevating the method into a game better penetrates consumer needs and priorities, particularly when exploring a complex space. Constant sum techniques are engaging by nature, and game play can be fun and exhilarating. That makes for high energy research well worth the up-front effort to create game boards.

The example that follows was designed for demonstration purposes only, showing a variety of ways to present attributes. More extensive game boards have been designed for consumables in categories with much less consumer involvement. An actual game for cars would be more extensive.

Some attributes, like the color of the car, only require the consumer to choose between equally weighted options. Often these characteristics are tangent to what's being explored, but they are critical to consumers decisions. So, they should be included.

Other characteristics are available in levels and at various prices. Players spend their chips on the higher-level options that are appealing to them. On this game board, a chip is spent for every cup holder or electric outlet.

There are four different alternatives for how the car is powered (gas, diesel, electric or hybrid). The route is slightly different if electric is chosen, since miles per gallon are irrelevant.

Some characteristics are optional. There are six different window options available in this example, from tinting to frost resistance. They can pick as of these as many as they want.

It can be insightful to include a block about the personality of the product, or an aspect of it (i.e. fragrance). It may reveal underlying emotional needs that they are trying to fulfill and reveal deeper motivations. The wheel on the board requests a division of chips that represents the personality of the car.

The pricing block is counter-intuitive on its face. It costs more chips to spend less. But that's because a player should have fewer chips to spend on the rest of the board if they want to get a low price.

Design your own vehicle

A leading automobile manufacturer is designing a new vehicle. It is important for the manufacturer to know what characteristics and features are important to you. On the board are many different characteristics and features that this vehicle can have. Your job is to divide **210** chips on the board to create best combination of benefits and design for your needs.

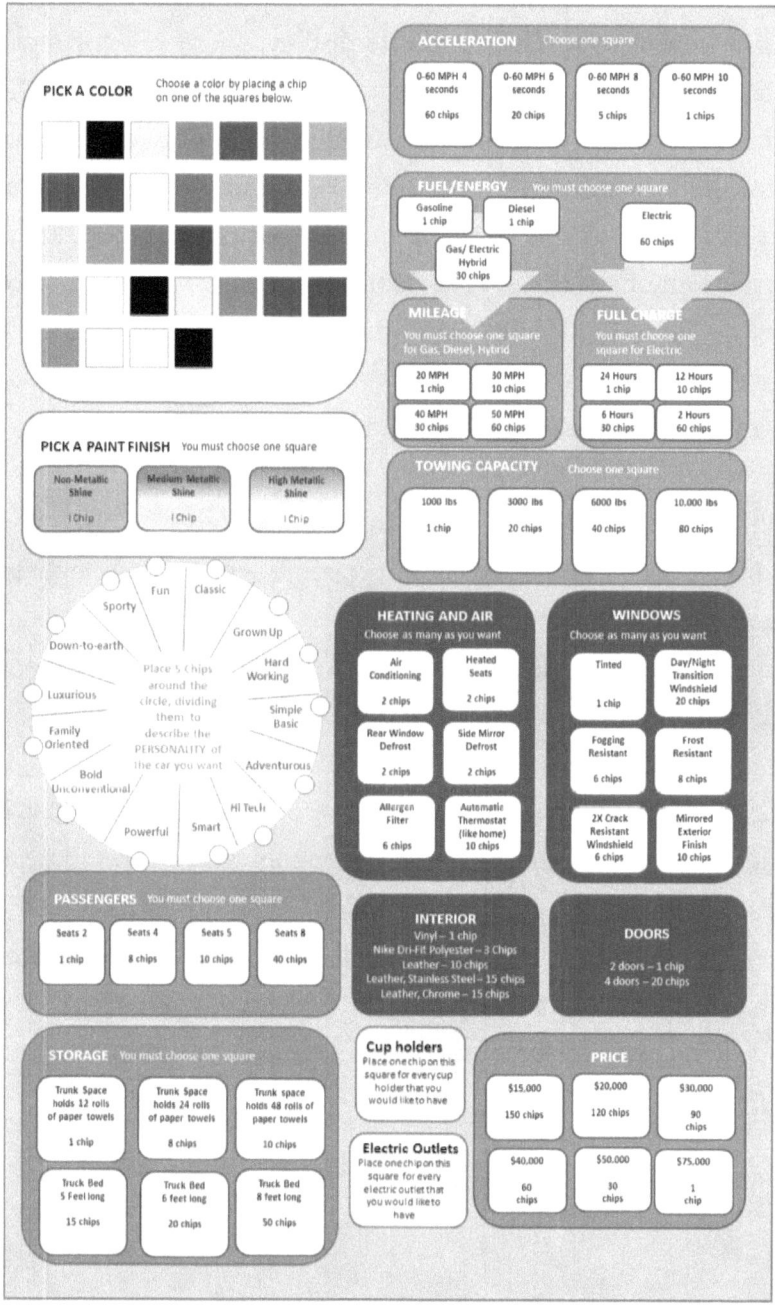

Designing Your Own Game

Make a list of all the possible benefits and characteristics that are relevant to consumers. Then generate options and levels for those attributes. Express options in common sense terms. In the example, trunk space options were defined by how many rolls of paper towels it would hold rather than in square feet, which is an abstract measure that is hard to grasp. Avoid using classifications to describe options (i.e., SUV, 4 door sedan, mini-van, etc.) since they bring assumptions and biases. Instead, include options for the distinguishing features of classifications. This allows a player to design a vehicle that doesn't neatly fit into known classes.

Next, think through the impact of these alternatives on the retail price. If you aren't an expert, talk to people who are… scientists, engineers and the people that will deliver the innovation to your consumer. You may delete a few blocks, modify others and tack on some new ones.

After drafting your game (it takes basic PowerPoint skills), test it yourself. Have your friends play it. Refine the game through trial and error, including the chip values and the total that is used in the game. Scarcity forces choice, so you'll want to give them fewer chips than it takes to get everything that's desired. Whatever any player designs for themselves should be feasible, or at least be in the realm of possibility.

Playing the game

A table sized board is ideal since it makes it feel more like a game. Print it out with a plotter printer and mount it onto illustration board. Meet with consumers one-on-one to play the game while you listen. Again, ask them to think out loud so that you understand what's important to them. You may have to prompt them a few times until they get into the flow of speaking their thoughts. Answer their questions if it's appropriate, but otherwise respond, "Well, what do you think?" Try to withhold your questions until they have finished; instead you can jot them down so you don't forget them. After 8 to 10 interviews, you will be thinking like your consumer and that understanding will be a compass to find the next Big Idea.

Needs: Naked Truths

If you are confident that you understand how consumers think, then you are ready to begin distilling your knowledge into Naked Truths about Needs. It's an undercurrent fact, problem or feeling that motivates actions and influences reactions. It's something that is REAL in the consumers' world. It can be a fact, a habit, a desire or a personal value.   *And* the reasons for it.   These phrases can prompt thinking.

> I am....
> I do...
> I believe...
> I have...
> .... And why.

It also contains the DEAL with that reality.   Not *how* they deal, but *the* deal. The definition of "deal" in the urban dictionary is "a fate that cannot be changed."   A deal is the "but" to the reality. These phrases may provoke thoughts:

> However...
> Yet...
> But...
> Except...

Here are a few examples:

I want to shine when I'm under pressure at work. That's when being at my best matters most. But stress causes sweat and odor that can keep me from looking and feeling confident. (deodorants)

I love long hair because it's so luxurious and sexy. But I wear it a little shorter than I'd like because it's easier to take care of and I don't have to worry about ugly fried ends. (female hair care)

I don't want to look old, since that's not who I am inside. But I'm afraid old is exactly how I look… and I'm hiding behind a mask I don't want to wear. (skin care, cosmetics)

I indulge myself every now and then, because it's the little luxuries in life that make it worth living. But I must take care of my family and if I spend too much on myself, I feel guilty. (general)

I want to encourage my kids to play outside and explore the world because I believe that developing their curiosity will help them be successful in life. At the same time, I find myself telling them not to touch things so they don't get sick. (hand sanitizing)

I get a dental cleaning twice a year, never miss a flossing, change brushes monthly and buy the best toothpaste to keep my teeth healthy. But my dentist just said I have to get another crown… WTF? Nobody takes better care of their teeth and I still have dental issues. (oral care)

Tips to Write Naked Truths about Needs

- Use the template below as a guide, not a rule. A Naked Truth can be articulated without using this format, perhaps more concisely, but this framework will make it easy.

- Write in the voice of consumers.

- Aim for fifty words or less.

- Focus on the ones that might be remedied.

- Cultivate a collection of 15 to 20 that inspire most.

REAL		DEAL
A Desire		
A Fact of Life	*And Why*	*But*
A Habit		
A Personal Value		

Remedies

There is no such thing as a perfect solution. It always comes at a cost of time, effort and/or money and has shortcomings which create new problems, sometimes a whole set of them.

Imperfection breeds streams of improvements by businesses trying to capture the market. It's the engine for progress. Successful innovation tends to broaden its use to applications for which it wasn't designed to meet, stemming new imperfections to address.

Computers were invented to compute, to solve complex mathematical problems that scientists found time consuming and subject to human error. Technology advanced and expanded their use, as well as what they were used for. Consumers bought calculators in the seventies, had desktops at work in the eighties, personal laptops in the nineties, surfed the web in the new millennium, and have smart phones today. Along the way, computers were integrated into everything from cars to bread makers, changing the way people live and work. It has birthed multibillion dollar industries and corporations, like video gaming entertainment, Google and Amazon. Computers have become an indispensable part of modern life.

Consider your innovation space and the remedies available to consumers to meet their needs. They may be using other products and adopting compensatory habits to deal with them, or choosing to do nothing at all. Imagine how to give them better solutions.

There are many companies that excel in progressing their categories and obsoleting existing solutions. Kraft Foods introduced Crystal Light low calorie drink mix in 1982. It was a successful brand, but Kraft discovered that people didn't always want to make a full pitcher, so it introduced "On the Go" packets in 2004. This transformed and grew the category. But it was still an effort to tear off the top and dissolve the powder in your water, so they launched Mio in 2011. The liquid form requires little mixing and the package design makes it convenient to carry. It's not premeasured so the consumer can make a lot or a little, at their preferred concentration. The market share of single serve packets is shrinking, evident in shelving at grocery stores.

Imperfections are Functional Problems

If the following list looks familiar, it's because it already appeared in the section on Human Needs. They are as valuable in diagnosing technology challenges as they are in understanding psychology.

Functional Problems

Barrier	Dissonance	Unknown
Risk	Gap	Inescapable Truth
Difference	Paradox	Conflict
Compromise	Incapability	Return on Investment
Imbalance	Complexity	Support
Compensate	Loss	Disorder
Control	Time	Consequences
Interruption	Effort	Unpredictable

On the Go packets address a functional problem of control. People wanted to be able to mix up a glass of Crystal light whenever and wherever they were. But the package was designed for making pitchers. It could be messy to scoop just enough to make a single glass, and it wasn't practical to take the whole package with you.

The list of functional problems can prompt thinking about your innovation space. Write down thoughts about each one, or gather a team to brainstorm. Chart responses of the group instead of the silent exercise recommended for consumer problems, since hearing other ideas tends to generate new connections.

Think in Parallels

Mio's competitive advantage is that it reduces the physical effort of mixing. The package provides a secondary advantage of better control too. It has a silicone dispensing valve that neatly squirts and then cuts off the stream of thin liquid concentrate. It offers leakage protection when carrying it in a pocket or purse too. This dispensing technology had been available for nearly thirty years and commonly found on shampoo and body wash bottles which were often stored on their caps. It finally came to food categories, condiments, because those bottles are often stored on their caps as well. Packaging engineers had to recognize the parallel between storing and dispensing shampoo and ketchup bottles, and ultimately dispensing Mio bottles.

Finding parallels for problems is enlightening. It can help in imagining whole new solutions, improve on one already in hand, or become a core element in messaging.

Experts can struggle to do this. Knowledge can be bound by metaphors, analogies and parallels that were discovered long ago. They function as the lens with which everything is viewed. Often these analogies are shared by peers, and even a vast community of experts. For example, dermatologists compare skin to a wall constructed with bricks and mortar. Cells are like bricks and lipids (fatty material) are the cement that holds them together. It's a great analogy that is easy to understand, which is why it's taught in high school. It's so good, that it can be hard to think of skin in any other way. But it is also limiting. It's hard to think of new ideas without a new mental model. It's also hard to leverage the analogy in skin cream communication to consumers. Women buy beauty creams to make them feel pretty, and a brick wall isn't.

Fruit has skin, suggesting a potential parallel. There are apples, oranges, kiwis and strawberries. But the peels aren't the same. An apple has a thin shiny layer. Kiwis are fuzzy. Seeds are visible on the skin of a strawberry.

Oranges vaguely resemble human skin. They are hesperidiums, as are grapefruit, lemons and limes. Comparing skin to hesperidium fruits lends a new thinking lens. Hesperidium peels keep moisture from leaving, just like skin. The wall analogy is oriented toward blocking anything from getting inside. So, the fruit peel analogy is about keeping in, the wall analogy about keeping out. It suggests a different problem, which could lead to alternative technical approaches to skin care. Visualizations with oranges could be explored to demonstrate the benefits of existing creams. Fruit is a friendlier analogy for consumers, opening possibilities for communication.

Five Whys

This is a simple exercise that can produce paradigm shifts for you and your team. Start by asking why the remedy is imperfect. Then ask why the answer to that question is happening. Ask it five times. It can identify the root of problems and the true challenge to be solved. "Five whys" can clarify consumer needs and Market Forces too.

Walk in Their Shoes

Experience the consumers' reality. Try the imperfect remedies that you are trying to replace. Adopt the habits of those who use them. This will help you appreciate how the products work, and don't work. It will plant personal perspective about what is important in solving the Needs.

I was once on a project to explore personal hygiene habits in Brazil. Habits and practices data said that many Brazilians showered three times a day. At first it was dismissed as the result of a poor translation in the questionnaire. But the same finding came back from another study. It didn't make sense...

... Until I visited Sao Paulo. It was hot, muggy and the buildings weren't air conditioned. The streets were grimy and public transportation was crowded. I found myself taking a shower in the morning, another before dinner, and a third before going to bed.

Beachcombing

Scan the list of action verbs in Appendix 2 and pick two or three that are best for describing major functional problems in your space. Pick two or three verbs for each problem. It's a long list, but it's a lot easier than skimming the dictionary.

Next, take your short list of action verbs and try to think of parallels outside of where you are working, where parallel solutions may already exist.

Let's take skin cream as an example. Consumers want to fight aging and the loss of elasticity is main cause of wrinkles. The problem could be remedied by *tightening* the skin, or could the *flex* be put back in the skin, or can the elasticity be *regenerated* in some way.

Spanx undergarments tighten your stomach using textile fibers that stretch and have high strength. So, can a skin cream work in the same way, forming over sagging skin to support it?

Muscles flex. People with muscles are in shape. To get in shape you have to follow a regimen of eating right and exercise. So, can a skin care regimen be designed with vitamins, nutrients and physical stimulation, perhaps with a physical device that delivers skin health?

Plants regenerate. Trees live for hundreds of years. They drop their leaves when the weather gets cold and regrow them in the spring. Leaves from hundred-year-old trees look the same as ones from saplings. So, can a cold exfoliant scrub treatment, either stored in the freezer before use or formulated with cooling sensate ingredients, chill inflamed skin cells to stimulate natural regenerative powers?

Remedies: Naked Truths

"If I had one hour to solve a problem, I'd spend the first 55 minutes defining it and 5 minutes thinking of solutions."

-   **Albert Einstein (Unconfirmed)**

Defining the problem in an actionable, provocative way can go a long way to solving it. Here are five tools that can help:

-   **Restate the Problem**
    Sometimes stating the problem from a different point of view can lead to breakthroughs. An executive got blank stares when he asked employees to brainstorm "ways to increase their productivity".   But he was flooded with suggestions when he changed his question to "ways to make their jobs easier".   Try writing at least 5 different statements to express your challenge.

-   **Liberate from Assumptions**
    Assumptions shroud every problem.   Assumptions dictate what can and can't be done. Some may come from obsolete belief systems or past experiences with failure.   These false assumptions can obscure a real issue.

    Find as many assumptions as you can, including the ones that "go without saying." Then poke at them. Look for situations and conditions in which they wouldn't be true. Some assumptions will be "sacred cows", self-imposed restrictions that don't have to be. For example, Apple would not have ventured into MP3 players with iPods if they had limited their space to personal computers.

- **Pull it Apart**

  Break the problem down into pieces. Several smaller or adjacent problems may be contributing to it. Deconstructing the problem into its components may lead to a more solvable, and impactful problem to tackle. Ask:

  > *"What are parts to this?"*
  > *"What are examples of this?"*
  > *"What's causing this?"*
  > *"What's getting in the way?*
  > *"What's making this worse?*

- **Bigger Picture**

  Just as every problem has parts to it; every problem is also part of larger one. Consider the Ptolemaic Astronomers working out fudge factors to fit data. Copernicus thought there was a bigger issue at work, that the fundamental model was wrong. So, try studying it from a higher altitude. Ask:

  > *"What's the larger issue?"*
  > *"What's the whole picture?"*
  > *"What's this an example of?"*
  > *"What's this an outgrowth of?"*
  > *"What's this a symptom of?"*

- Flip the Problem

  Reversing the problem statement can provoke insight and understanding. For example, skin scientists want to *prevent* wrinkles. It could help to change the problem to *making* wrinkles. That may identify various contributing factors that had not been considered yet.

Naked Truths about Remedies consist of a primary underlying problem and it cause, plus a way to alleviate it. Strive for solutions based in analogies or parallels. They are powerful because they 1) express a mechanism in a few words, and 2) are proven with the potential for reapplication.

UNDERLYING PROBLEM	SOLUTION	
The primary issue with today's remedies and what causes it.	*Eliminate it by . . .* *Work around it by . . .*	*And How*

To illustrate, here is Mio's Naked Truth:

UNDERLYING PROBLEM	SOLUTION
To Go Packets must be shaken vigorously in water before drinking, because they are powder.	*Let's invent a new liquid concentrate form. Use packaging dispensing technology used for squeezable ketchup bottles, in a miniature form.*

Tips to write Naked Truths for Remedies

- Use the template as a guide, not a rule. A Naked Truth can be articulated without using this format, perhaps more concisely, but this framework will make it easy.

- Aim for fifty words or less.

- Write in the voice of an entrepreneur.

- Simple language.

- One problem and one solution per Naked Truth.

- Remedies are different from one another even if they have the same problem, as long as they are coupled with a different solution.

- Cultivate a collection of 15 to 20 that inspire most.

Reverse Engineering

If the challenge is to find a Big Idea for an existing product or service, or a new technology nearing launch, then the approach to Remedy Naked Truths is slightly different. Start by articulating how the solution works in provocative, analogical ways. Go beyond baked-in explanations, like bricks and mortar in the skin care example. Explore all aspects of the technology, product or service.

Don't accept baked solutions "as is." That is to say, beware of accepting what developers are most proud of achieving as the most compelling aspect of the innovation. There may be something else about it, or a different way of describing it, that will be more inspirational for a Big Idea.

After studying the solution, use the list of functional problems to identify all the issues, and alternative definitions of the issues, that are remedied.

Market Forces

When exploring a new landscape, what you don't know can bite you. An entrepreneurial team was looking for new businesses opportunities, outside of the large company's current portfolio. One member suggested windshield washer fluid. At the time, all that was available at Walmart were blue jugs. The jugs were filled with colored water and little ethanol to prevent freezing in the winter. It actually didn't clean as well as plain water, so the market seemed ripe for a premium tier. There were over 200 million cars on the road, so if two gallons of fluid a year were sold to just a quarter of those cars, it would be a huge new business. The team got to work on a washer fluid formula and started concept development. It was an exciting time for them!

It was weeks before Finance broke the bad news. The manufacturers who made the blue fluid that was stocked on Walmart shelves would not be the biggest obstacle to success. It turned out that most people in warm regions fill their tanks with a hose, since they don't have freezing weather. People in dry climates don't buy much fluid because a gas station squeegee does just fine, for as often as they want it. Service garages across America top off the fluids during oil changes, which squelch refilling even more.

The existing retail market was less than $50 million in size. The team's perspective was skewed by living in a region where road salt is spread during the winter months, driving high consumption. The dynamics of the market made investment in windshield wash innovation much less attractive, so the effort was abandoned. That's not to say that it wouldn't be attractive to another company, just that it didn't meet the criteria that the large company had set.

When working in a familiar landscape, what you know can blind you. Opportunities may be dismissed if they don't fit with proven business models. If not dismissed, propositions can inadvertently be twisted to fit the mold of the "right way" to do things. Really bad ideas look better than they are. Just because there is the ability to do something, doesn't mean it should be done. American Kitchen had equipment to process dehydrated potatoes into oven fries. It could be employed to form anything into the shape of a fry. So, they introduced a line of vegetables disguised as French fries. "I hate peas" fries briefly appeared in the frozen food section in the seventies and the company that made them doesn't seem to be in business any more.

Archetypes

Karl Jung said that an archetype is a collectively inherited unconscious idea, pattern of thought, image, etc., that is universally accepted in individual psyches. They have grown in importance because consumers are bombarded with more information than ever. An archetype can be recognized in a blink, which may be all the time consumers are willing to put into making a choice.

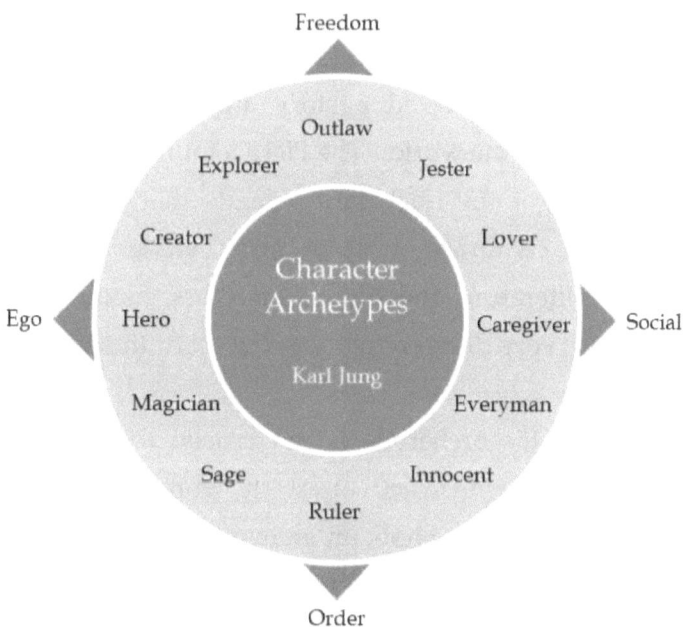

If you have been trained in marketing, then you may be familiar with Jung's character archetypes. Each type has a distinct personality that is universally recognized, which is what makes them valuable in creating brand identities that appeal to consumers. Iconic brands have personalities which are readily identified on the wheel: Nike is a hero, Harley Davidson the outlaw, Dove the caregiver.

The Hero with a Thousand Faces

Some are uncomfortable with the concept of archetypes. They are misunderstood as formulaic, restrictive or unoriginal. Joseph Campbell's book "The Hero with a Thousand Faces" shows that the opposite is true.

Joseph Campbell discovered a story archetype after comparing myths from around the world. The Hero's Journey is found, at least in part, in most of the important legends that had been passed down through centuries. It is also evident in classic and contemporary literature and film. Star Wars, Finding Nemo and Tommy Boy are very different movies, but all fit the pattern.

Joseph's Campbell's archetype is not crucial to create Big Ideas (although it can be instructive), so it won't be detailed here. However, it demonstrates how an archetype can be a creative tool. One archetype, thousands of different stories.

Realm Archetypes

Compare automobile ads you've seen lately. Maybe there was a car being driven on a winding mountain road, or through a city at night, or in a stark lab under the watch of techs with clipboards, or in a barren desert twisting around orange cones. These settings are common because they communicate to consumers in meaningful ways.

Take a walk down the cereal aisle. You'll see boxes with cartoon characters (i.e., Count Chocula), others displaying natural and organic pedigrees (i.e., Kashi), and still others with claims stolen from the pharmacy section (i.e. Fiber One). There is also a no-frills group (i.e. Shredded Wheat).

These are Realm Archetypes for automobiles and cereal. Look for Realms in the marketplace that you are exploring. There may be one or a handful. Realms are valuable for understanding dynamics that are at play in a space.

A Realm Archetype has four parts:

- It takes place in/on....

- It starts with...

- Its heart is a...

- Elements of the story include...

The four prominent Realms in beauty care are a good illustration. Successful brands in the category tend to fit these narratives, or a hybrid of several. Here is brief synopsis:

Science

Brands that have done it well: Pantene, L'Oréal

It takes place in a laboratory.
The story starts with a problem.
A mechanism is at the heart of the story.

Other elements:
Proven, advanced, men in white lab coats, magnitudinal claims (i.e. 3X)
Transformation, a struggle between your self-image and your physical self

Nature

Brands that have done it well: Aveda, Herbal Essences

It takes place in a virgin land.
The story starts with an ingredient.
Its heart has a higher calling.

Other elements:
Purity, knowing, plants, alternatives, escape, % claims, health & well-being

Signature

Brands that do it well: Super premium salon and fragrance brands

It takes place in a palace.
The story starts with a charismatic person.
Its heart is a romantic vision.

Other elements: Customized, professional, complete, luxury, creative, influential, worldwide

Ideal

Brands that do it well: CoverGirl, Revlon

It takes place on a stage.
The story starts with a Venus.
A supportive community is at its heart.

Other elements: Advice on how to, the latest style, admiration, being in the know, belonging, show and tell

The Code of the Nature Realm

For more detail in the example, let's delve deeper into the Nature Realm, since the archetype transcends the beauty marketplace. It can be found in food, restaurants, vitamins, clothing and many other consumer goods. A code has developed around the archetype which has four parts:

- **Substance**

    Nature stories begin with ingredients. Often the ingredients are reassuring since they seem familiar, which evokes experiences, memories and comfort. It's easy to picture what they are, or at least what they would be like. Ingredients are familiar, but not common. Common is boring, generic and hurt the impressions about potency and value.

    Missing substances can be part of the story (i.e., Gluten-Free", "no artificial ingredients"), but they can't be the focus. The Nature Realm is experiential, and you can't experience something that isn't there.

    Vocabulary: Specific botanical ingredient or mineral, oil, crème, concentrate, essence, extract, serum

- **Source**

    The origins of ingredients are important in the nature realm. The place should be un-modernized (i.e., the Amazon rainforest) and can refer to ancient times. Products may be made with a human touch (handcrafted, hand-picked) or without one (i.e., grown in virgin soil). The people behind the company have a higher calling (i.e., healthier living, preserving the environment, ending poverty in third world countries).

Vocabulary: Un-modernized geographic location, hand-made, handcrafted, responsible, mission, genuine, naturally derived, countless years.

- **Science**

  Scientific terms build potency impressions. Science tests the ingredients, but does not alter them in any way. An ingredient's mode of action can be described in technical terms (i.e., "Ginkgo Biloba is an antioxidant") or measured in technical tests (i.e., clinical trials).

  Vocabulary: Botanical, vitamins, protein, aminos, complex, organic, balance, super, beta, omega, hydrating, immunity boosting, antioxidant, promoting, bio___, phyto___.

- **Standards**

  A reputable third party gives its stamp of approval and its certifications are prominently featured. Claims are stated in percentages (i.e., 100% certified organic) rather than magnitude (i.e., 5 times stronger).

  Vocabulary: Organic, pure, 100%, whole, all natural, certified, royal, select, essential, clinically proven, premium.

Explore the Nature Realm for yourself. Look for the archetype and its code at Starbucks, Whole Foods Market, Aveda or any brand offering natural oriented products. You can visit them online:

www.starbucks.com
www.wholefoodsmarket.com

www.aveda.com

How to Identify Marketplace Realms

Examine the products and services being offered in your space. Look in the stores, the websites, and watch videos on YouTube. Cluster what you observe. It may help to lay brands out on a map to display crossover into more than one realm. Back in the cereal aisle, shredded wheat lives in the "no frills" realm, but blueberry Mini-Wheats has one foot in cartoon land. Once you have identified the pure, core realms, give them a name. Identify similarities in attitude, imagery and vocabulary for each group. Then utilize the four-part framework to articulate the Realm clearly.

Trends

"Trend" refers to the general direction that something is developing or changing. A trend can be found in observations of technical data, demographics, the stock market or and a myriad of other topics. In consumer goods and services, it has a particular meaning: a symbiotic development occurring between consumers and manufacturers/ providers. It is a pattern in innovation that is feeding the appetite of consumers.

Trends are paramount for market understanding. They are newsworthy. Learn about them on trend blogs, books, magazine articles and TED talks. A lot of people put a lot of time into documenting them. Although you may serendipitously recognize them, *you don't have to spot them yourself.* Study the information that is out there and search for signs of them in your space.

Successful innovation addresses drivers of a trend, or its consequences, rather than the trend itself. These undercurrents are often not well understood or misdiagnosed. So that is where trend analysis and critical thinking is beneficial.

The trend of instant gratification is well documented. It is the latest manifestation of a time savings movement that has been a strong current since the beginning of the industrial revolution. This trend takes saving time into no-wait options and solutions, from texting to Google searches to binge watching TV shows. "Fast-lane" premium passes can be purchased at amusement parks. Amazon is striving for same day delivery.

Time starvation is often cited as a key driver of this trend; that people don't have enough time. Quantitative reinforcement is not hard to find. People aren't getting enough sleep. 68% of US adults have trouble falling asleep (Consumer Reports, 5/2015). 30% get less than 6 hours of sleep (National Health Interview Survey, 2010). People cope by multitasking, demonstrated by what they do in their cars. 41% have eaten breakfast, lunch or dinner while driving in the past year (Pew Research, 2010). 61% of drivers text, 33% email, 28% surf the net while driving (AT&T, 5/2015).

But the force that is driving instant gratification is surprising: people want to accomplish as much as they can. Getting stuff done makes them feel good, even if it's not essential to do it.

People are busy, but busy by choice. It's is something to brag about. "How have you been?" is asked. "I've been busy!" is replied. If you haven't been busy, it's best not to admit it. 57% pretend to be busier than they really are (Havas Worldwide, 9/2015). If you're not busy, you're not successful; you are not as important as someone who is busy.

This force makes waiting intolerable. It's lost time that could have been spent doing something productive. Consumers are more impatient today. They want what they want on demand. Any innovation which saves time is welcomed, but that time won't be spent on sleeping in. It will be used to get more stuff done, and that's what makes instant results meaningful today. Not to release us from the burden of our tasks, but give us the capacity to tote a bigger burden.

The aim of innovation speaking to instant gratification should be to enable everyone to accomplish more. It's a higher order goal than providing instant results. That higher altitude will provide vison about what's next and not just what's now.

A wave of innovation that enables multitasking could be what's next. Multitasking is a compensating behavior that fills time better. It can feel like it's being more efficient, even if it isn't. Have you ever seen someone pull out of drive thru at five mph because they are trying to eat their burger while they drive? They really aren't saving time, and they aren't being safe, but it feels faster.

Multitasking means that tasks are done with divided attention. We want innovation that removes the necessity to concentrate, study instructions, or monitor the process. There is an appetite for microwaves that would sense when food is fully heated so there's no reason to stand around and wait for them to finish. Apps that translate speech into text would solve the issues with texting and driving.

Business Realities

The strengths, weaknesses and limitations of your company should also be considered Market Forces. Perhaps there is a proprietary advantage in technology that can be applied to the space. There could be track record of success in certain types of initiatives, indicating organization skills that could be leveraged. On the other hand, maybe there is a referendum on capital expenses that must be considered. Maybe your company doesn't have experience with the prevailing business models in the space. Consider internal assets and challenges to achieving goals.

Market Forces: Naked Truths

One part of Naked Truths for Market Forces is a dynamic being observed in the space or your business. It's a movement that is rising or one that is falling. It can also be a phenomenon that is unchanging. These phrases may prompt thinking:

> ... is rising
> ... is falling
> ... is strengthening

… is weakening
… is preventing
… is immovable
… is growing
… is dying
… is eating
… is being eaten

… and why

The second part is a potential response:

Ride the dynamic by…
Counter the dynamic by…

… and how

Let's revisit the windshield washer fluid story to formulate a Market Force. Consumers will continue to have fluid reservoirs topped off during oil changes. That dynamic is an immovable force that will continue to eat into the volume of retails sales.

Interestingly, service shops offer customers standard and premium packages, better oil for a few dollars more. What if they were supplied with superior washer fluid too, then they could raise the price of their premium service or have more success trading up their customers. Dealers could be convinced to recommend using only premium fluid. Awareness of the premium fluid's benefits would grow over time, and that could propel a future retail introduction.

Tips to Write Naked Truths for Forces

- Use the template below as a guide, not a rule. A Naked Truth can be articulated without using this format, perhaps more concisely, but this framework will make it easy.

- Aim for fifty words or less.

- Write in the voice of an entrepreneur

- Simple language

- Cultivate a collection of 15 to 20 that most inspire.

DYNAMIC		RESPONSE	
What is Rising *What is Falling* *What is Unchanging*	*And Why*	*Ride it by . . .* *Counter it by . . .*	*And How*

Here's is a Force Truth written for windshield wash:

DYNAMIC	RESPONSE
Service garages and dealers fill windshield washer fluid during routine maintenance.	*Partner with dealers and major service chains to include premium fluid with their premium service.*

Case Study – Part 2

Jack was discouraged about finding a Big Idea for Acme, but was impressed with the factory's quality control and candy making know-how.   He believed that Acme had the equipment and expertise to make anything.

Jack asked some of his friends and coworkers about their thoughts and feelings about candy.   Everyone had a love-hate relationship. Candy tastes good, but it's not good for you.   He heard:

> *I used to eat a couple of chocolate bars a day. It was a nice boost of energy when I needed it. But I can't do that anymore, I'd be as big as a house.*

> *Candy isn't good for you because it spikes your blood sugar and rots your teeth. But I treat myself every once in a while.*

I reach for candy when I'm stressed. That's why I don't keep it in the house anymore. Although I've been known to raid candy dishes at work.

Jack went grocery shopping with his family and noticed a few things about candy. His new assignment gave him a set of new antennas. Here was some of what he saw:

Chocolate is everywhere now... it's in cereal, yogurt and granola bars. Maybe perceptions are changing about candy not being good for you. He wonders if other kinds of candy can be added to healthy foods.

Sports drinks are growing in the beverage aisles, perhaps due to being viewed as a healthier drink than traditional sugared beverages. He wonders how candy can become part of this trend... how can candy be crossed with sports drinks?

There is a lot of chewy candy with wild and unusual flavors, even gross ones. It's brings to mind the Disney mantra, "Fear – Death = Fun." He wonders if Acme can create new candy experiences.

The organic section was bigger than he remembered, almost like a store within a store. He saw chocolate covered organic dried fruit and wondered if the was an opportunity for other forms of organic candy.

Jack was beginning to see opportunities, and he now suspected that there is at least one Big Idea out there. He ran some qualitative research with men, women and children in which he conducted a constant sum exercise. Participants divided ten bingo chips among a list of characteristics, based on how they wanted to improve their favorite candy.

Tastes better	Gives you more energy
More nutritious	Better for your teeth
More flavors	More healthy
Less calories	More natural
Easier to take with you	

It was surprising to find that men, women and kids had different priorities:

Men wanted better tasting candy that gave them more energy. Many considered chocolate to be their favorite and liked that chocolate had caffeine, like coffee. One guy said that there should be "Expresso shot chocolate for adults and Decaf for kids". Some had tried energy bars, but didn't like the flavor as much as "normal" candy. They also allotted a few chips to healthier candy, although they didn't want fewer calories because that is what gave them energy.

> *Chocolate is like a cup of coffee in the afternoon since it wakes me up. But once the sugar rush fades in an hour or so, I actually feel more tired.*

Women loved chocolate. One lady said, "Chocolate makes me happy." They wanted less calories and more natural ingredients; except several said that candy would have to be 100% natural or it wouldn't matter to them.   Many paid attention to wrappers and disliked the long lists of ingredients they found there, which indicated lots of preservatives and being unhealthy. The wrapper was checked for calories, although one lady said, "I know it's bad, so I don't want to know." Interestingly, several women weren't interested in better taste because it was already their favorite candy, "so why change it?"

> *Chocolate is a guilty pleasure because I crave it knowing it has lots of calories and artificial ingredients that aren't good for me. If there was a Chocoholics Anonymous, I would be a member.*

Kids wanted better taste and more flavors. They also wanted candy to be more nutritious so that their moms would let them eat it more often.   Jack asked some mothers how they felt about kids eating candy, specifically seeing other kids eating candy.   "I know it's wrong to judge anyone this way," one lady said. "But I wonder if their mother pays attention to what they are eating, or if she even cares."

> *Limiting the amount of sweets my kids eat is one way that I show I love them. I search for healthy alternatives that they like.*

The one-on-ones sparked new questions about the market place and the Acme Candy Company. Finance provided some perspective. Hershey and Mars/Wrigley have about 60% of the market, with Hershey leading the chocolate market and Mars/Wrigley on top of chewy candy market.   There are more than three hundred candy manufacturers in the United States.

Candy and gum is the third biggest food category, trailing only milk and carbonated beverages. Chocolate is America's favorite confection, comprising almost 60% of the Market. Gum represents 10% of the market with the remaining share divide among non-chocolate candies. Chewy candy and licorice is the fastest growing sweets segment and represents about half of all non-chocolate candy sales.

He reads an on-line article about four major trends in the category: Organic, Convenience/Portability, Vitamin Fortified and Low Cal/Fat/Sugar. The author said:

> "People are eating fewer balanced meals because hectic lifestyles have eroded traditional eating patterns. People want healthy meal alternatives that let them eat whenever and wherever they are."

He thought this statement wasn't quite right based on what he remembered in his qualitative research. So, he revised it as a Force Truth:

> *People are eating fewer balanced meals because hectic lifestyles have eroded traditional eating habits. People want healthy meal ~~alternatives~~ BRIDGES that let them eat whenever and wherever they are.*

Next, he visited the grocery store again and found that most candies had about twenty ingredients. Twix had the most, more than a Cheeto, with 27. He walked through the beverage section on his way out, and was struck by its similarities to the candy aisle. They both displayed bright colors and bold branding. Cans of pop were boxed; just as wrapped candy was bagged. Except that the beverages market was more developed. It occupied more space and there were more non-flavor sub-segments, like sports drinks, and energy drinks. There were also dietary alternatives, like diet, caffeine free and low sodium. He had found another Force Truth:

> *Beverages have non-flavor sub segments to better meet the functional and dietary needs and desires of their consumers. The future of the candy could be to evolve the aisle in the same way.*

Jack called Bill, one of the employees that had impressed him at Acme, and shared what he had learned. Bill gave him new perspective about the production competencies at Acme. They followed old fashioned recipes, so many of the ingredients were already naturally sourced. The recipes were simple; rock candy was made with two ingredients, granulated cane sugar and water.

> *Modern candy is made with a lot of ingredients, some of which is highly processed and artificial. Modern manufacturing techniques and the cost and availability of raw materials demand it. Acme makes old fashioned styled candies in small batches that are simply made with natural ingredients.*

Acme candy makers had expertise in a wide range of candy, unlike what might be found at a major brand's manufacturing facility. They made over a hundred different candies in small batches. So, if Jack had an idea for a new candy, they could probably make it for him.

3: CONNECT

The path to a Big Idea is a labyrinth. New clues or dead ends are behind every door. The maze is not traveled blindly. Good intuition is a factor in success... intuition that is based on knowledge, not a paranormal sixth sense. Naked Truths illuminate the way.

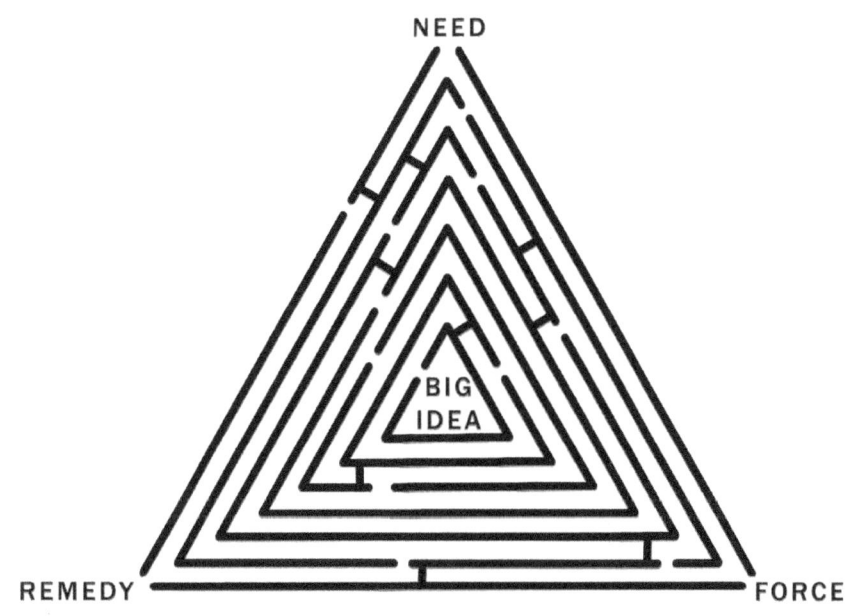

The Discover phase should have surfaced Naked Truths in abundance. But they may still only be a fragment of the big picture. The aim of Connect is to find linkages between the initial collections of Naked Truths and knowledge that has yet to be leveraged. Ultimately, Connection will produce more Naked Truths that run deeper and wider.

Think of Needs, Remedies and Forces as three buckets. There are two distinct activities in Connection, 1) looking inside a bucket for deeper meaning beyond what has already been learned, and 2) making connections across buckets to identify how some Naked Truths are tied together.

Napkin Models

"Napkin models" are a tool to look deeper into each bucket. They can be sketched out on a napkin to reveal the invisible rules that govern the space. They help in three ways: 1) revealing more Naked Truths about your space, 2) making sense of disconnected, even contradictive information, and 3) organizing and editing your knowledge into a communicative form. Consumer needs, psychology and behaviors are usually more complex, layered and tangled than the other buckets. Therefore, put at least twice as much thinking into analyzing the Need Truth bucket to find deeper meaning.

There are seven kinds of models, all of which can be employed for articulating rules and meaning of Consumer Needs, Market Forces or Remedies. However, given the complexity involved with the Need bucket; only consumer examples are covered.

Story

Tell a story to illustrate an insight. This is a simple form of model, so much so that it can be done without a napkin. For example:

> *When I feel a headache coming on, I take three Extra Strength Motrin to knock it out. Then I take another dose an hour earlier than the recommended time to make sure it doesn't come back. My wife, on the other hand, waits till she has a full-blown headache before she takes half an aspirin. Then if it isn't gone in two days, she takes the other half. I am an aggressive medicator; my wife is a passive medicator.*

Story models are "sticky"; people remember them. That's an advantage when trying to unite a team around an idea, because they don't need a PowerPoint slide to jog their memory while doing their jobs. Try inventing a story for one of your Naked Truths.

Breakdown

A breakdown model takes an abstract, subjective or emotional quality and breaks it up into measurable attributes. It deconstructs the subject into its components, and then into the components of the components. It is a skill possessed by most scientists and engineers.

Engineers used breakdown models to transform the Japanese auto industry in the 1950s and 60s, with the influence of William Deming. American consumers said they wanted quality cars. This was unclear to Japanese engineers, so they investigated consumers' perceptions of quality, like the sound a door makes when it's shut. The sound was quantified and written into specifications that reproduced it in Japanese cars. Specifications were devised for all the attributes that signaled quality.

A "Consumer Chore Model" appears on the next page. Let's start at the top. That's where positive emotional motivators appear, but they are less important than the negative motivators. The worth of success is outweighed by the frustration of failure because success is expected.

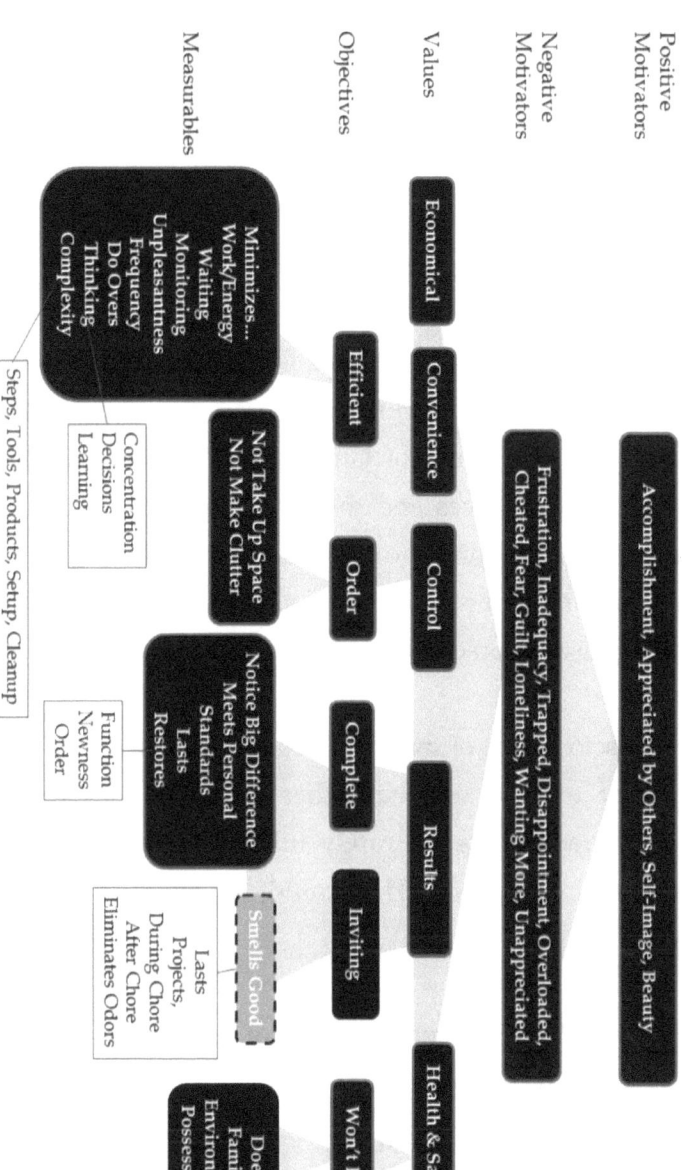

Consumer Chore Model

Unexpected failures are the worry, and they are surrounded with negative emotions.

A noteworthy insight in the next section is that chores should end in complete, inviting results. The result of cooking is a good meal, and it should be inviting to the family in every way. A clean-living room will be inviting to guests.

Smelling good is a shaded attribute. It's valued by consumers, both during and after chores. However, it is not part of all tasks. It's essential to the experience of laundry and cleaning the bathroom, but not for raking leaves and mowing the lawn. This infers that there may be opportunities to infuse noticeable fragrance into other chores. Car care is one possibility, where scented car wax and air-freshening plastic protectant may have appeal.

The subconscious aim of many chores is to restore newness. Clean is an aspect of newness, but other attributes can be involved. Newness characteristics are rarely fully quantified, just as quality had not been for cars. This could be an avenue for deeper exploration.

Efficiency has been a central theme of innovation in this space. Minimizing physical work and effort, reducing complexity, sparing mental energy and shaving time from chores have all been embraced by consumers. Less waiting links to the Instant Gratification trend in Chapter 2.

Breakdown models are relevant to most spaces. Start with a benefit, state, attribute or judgement value and identify everything that would contribute to it. Then examine all the contributors and what contributes to them. Continue breaking down each factor until you reach technically measurable characteristics.

Level

This type is best for prioritizing competing attributes. Maslow's Hierarchy of Needs is an example of this framework.

Maslow's Hierarchy of Needs

Abraham Maslow divided human needs into five levels. Physiological needs were the most basic. "Self-actualization" or "self-transcendence" needs were the highest order. Maslow contended that people satisfy each level of needs before graduating to higher order needs. To illustrate, someone with bleeding gums will seek a remedy to alleviate their pain before considering a whitening treatment.

Stage

This framework depicts anything that progresses, transforms or follows a path. The Transtheoretical Model of Behavioral Change illustrates this. It is the foundation of many addiction breaking programs, such as Alcoholics Anonymous Twelve Step Program. A notable insight from the model is that unhealthy behaviors can't be ended without healthy ones to replace them.

Although conceived for combating addiction, it is valuable for planning the launch of any innovation that requires a habit change, or any existing product that wishes to grow its consumption.

- **Stage 1: Precontemplation -** People at this stage are not thinking of changing their behavior, and may be unaware of the need to change. They usually undervalue the pros for changing and underestimate the cons if they continue their destructive habits.

- **Stage 2: Contemplation –** At this stage, people have become aware of the need to form new habits and intend to adopt healthy behaviors in the near future. While they see the pros of changing, they don't outweigh the cons in their mind. This ambivalence can cause them to procrastinate.

Transtheoretical Model of Change

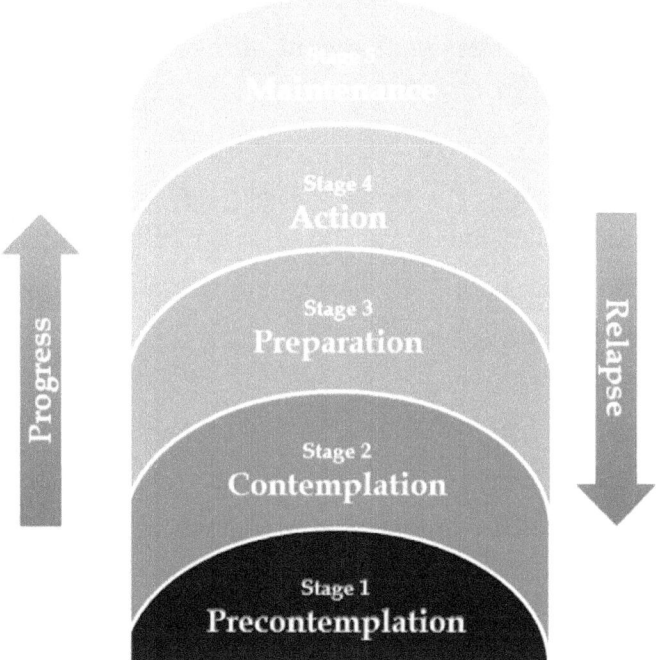

- **Stage 3: Preparation -** They are ready to take action soon. They take small steps that they believe can help them make the advantageous behavior a part of their lives. Removing temptations from their environment is one way. Commitment can be cemented by telling friends and family that they want to make a change.

- **Stage 4: Action –** These people have changed their behavior recently, but have not fully formed new habits. They fight urges to slip back into old, destructive ways and learn that old habits die hard.

- **Stage 5: Maintenance** - People at this stage have adopted new, beneficial habits. They should have become aware, and avoid, situations and stresses that could trigger reversion to negative actions.

- **Stage 6: Relapse** – This stage describes anyone who changed their unhealthy behavior and reached the maintenance stage, but had resumed it. In relapse, these individuals may slip back into any of the earlier stages.

Classification

The classification framework is the most versatile. It can provide clarity and detail for anyone who receives a Big Idea and must execute or create with it. Layers of knowledge can be added to classification constructs, like adding information to a file. How individual classifications fit with one another is not included, or at least de-emphasized.

Rogers' lays out technology adoption model in Diffusion of Innovation first published in 1962. It is a nice illustration of a classification model. It divides the population five groups.

- **Innovators**

  Innovators are first to adopt an innovation. They are aware of the latest developments and are the first in line to buy them, accepting that there is some risk to being the first triers. These connoisseurs are a tiny part of the population and can be extreme users that are dissimilar from average consumers, but are very social and often have close ties to the industry.

- **Early Adopters**

  These are the second fastest to adopt an innovation. Like innovators, they tend to be better educated, enjoy higher social status and have more discretionary income. They also tend to be at the center of their social circle. Having or doing the latest thing helps maintain their social standing, its social currency for them. They communicate about their experiences with innovation, so pleasing them is critical to business success.

  Talk to these folks if you are trying to change habits. They approach innovation with an open mind, but won't fall for fads or flawed solutions that lack value. Note that someone who is an early adopter in one space may not be in another. Imagine a video gaming enthusiast who has Samsung Gear VR (Virtual Reality), but always buys Old Spice deodorant since that's what his dad bought.

- **Early Majority**

  Adoption takes place sometime after the innovators and early adopters have opted in. They are not opinion leaders like innovators and early adopters, but they often know them.

- **Late Majority** These individuals approach an innovation with a high degree of skepticism and only adopt after most of society already has.

- **Laggards**

  Individuals in this category are the last to adopt an innovation. These consumers are typically older and have an aversion to change. They may only adopt when their usual product has become obsolete and unavailable.

Map

The Kano model depicts how consumers react to different kinds of benefits and features. Let's look at automobiles to explain. People expect windshields to come with the car. Having a crystal-clear windshield doesn't raise satisfaction with the car, but not having one, or having one that's scratched and hazy would be extremely dissatisfying. Having a windshield is a *basic* benefit.

Gas mileage varies from car to car. Better mileage improves satisfaction. It's a significant criterion for choosing a car, which is why it is printed on the price sticker on the window. It's a *performance* benefit.

Delighter benefits are unexpected and not previously known to consumers. Imagine test driving a new car and suddenly experiencing a shiatsu massage which is automatically activated if it senses tight back muscles. That could be a feature that would improve your impression of the car, even if it wasn't the best massage you'd ever gotten. That innovation isn't here yet, but Stanford University and auto parts manufacturer Faurecia are working on it.

Kano Model of Consumer Satisfaction

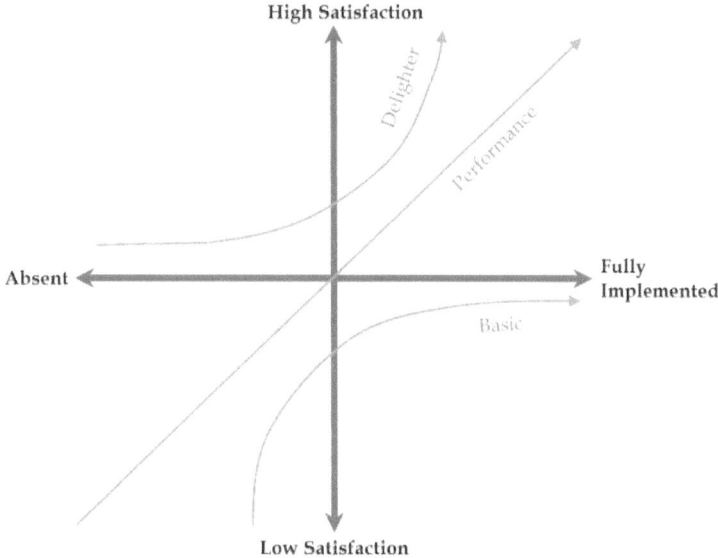

Delighter opportunities arise from observations of consumer behavior, seeing what is useful rather than asking what is desired.

"If I had asked people what they wanted, they would have said faster horses."

- (Attributed to) Henry Ford

The model also maintains that benefits evolve over time from delighter to basic benefits as consumers become accustomed to having them. Automobiles didn't have windshields until 1904. Power windows were introduced on luxury models in the 1940s. Now all cars have them, including economy models.

Graphs are often leveraged for consumer segmentation. They make classifications and compare them to each other, displaying how they differ and where there is overlap.

To practice making Map models, try creating one for your market space. Write all the brands, stores or products onto individual Post-it notes. Arrange them on a wall or tabletop, placing similar ones together and unlike ones apart. The most unlike groups should be farthest from each other. Name any natural groupings that you see. Look at the groupings that are spaced farthest apart from one another. In what way are they opposites? This may suggest a vector. Are there other ways that groupings are opposite? This might form other vectors. This is also called affinity diagramming.

Analogical

Metaphors and analogies can be employed to create concise, memorable models. For example, there are three ways that pet owners approach nutrition for their dogs. Some owners see their dog as *a member of the family* with human needs and desires. They are likely to feed them food from the dinner table and buy cans with ingredients they would serve in a family meal. Other owners feed their dog like *an athlete*. Their dog may be a purebred with papers. They buy specialized nutrition that is fortified with vitamins for peak health and condition. Lastly, some owners view their dog as *an animal* that depends on them. They don't have strong emotional bond with their dog, like the other two types of owners have. They believe all dog foods provide adequate nutrition, so they buy brands that their pets like and are a good value.

Analogical models can be incorporated into other forms. You might be sketching a level model and think, "it's like climbing a mountain!" Or you'll look at your stage diagram and notice that, "it's like running a marathon!" Models can be strengthened and made more memorable by weaving an analogy into the visualization or into the story you share when you explain it.

Making a Napkin Model

Examine the Naked Truths that you've drafted. Look at each bucket of Truths separately.

- What must you understand better to be successful?

- Do you see any recurring themes in Needs? How about in the Forces or Remedies?

- Which Truths are different facets of the same thing? What can the "thing" be called?

- Is there anything that deserves more depth and exploration than the Truths provide?

- Are there any contradictory Naked Truths?

The opportunities for modeling will be abundant. Prioritize the top one or two and draw your thoughts on paper. Try out several types of models to capture what you know in a simple way.

Once you've got something that you like, let it inspire more Naked Truths.

Quantitative Research

If you are fortunate to have the financial resources to conduct large base quantitative research with consumer, then you can investigate your space with statistics. Factor analysis can be readily translated into classification and map models. Regression and Bayesian networks simulate how variables influence one another which can be turned into breakdown models. Statistical analyses are not just for consumer research; they can isolate the most important attributes that drive market and technical results as well.

However, a model is only as good as the data, and data is only as good as what is measured. This is particularly true in consumer research where insight is necessary to ask the right questions. It can seem expedient to place quantitative studies without doing qualitative research prior to designing questionnaires. But that jeopardizes the quality and actionability of the tests. Synthesize napkin models as research hypotheses *before* composing questionnaires. Write questions that will validate or dismiss your Naked Truths and measure the size or influence of the elements of your models.

In organizations with mature understanding, the same questions can be asked year after year. It's not ideal since, 1) the Kano model shows that consumer acceptance is dynamic and changes over time, 2) competitive solutions are continuously and changing, 3) organization knowledge of the consumer should also be growing, so new understanding should be sought and 4) consumer needs, taste and style can shift.

"Moisture" was a dirty word in hair care in the 1980s. Consumers thought moisture would weigh down their hair, so it was a big turn-off in any communication. Flash forward fifteen years and "moisture" had become one of the most attractive benefits to consumers. Dove, with a moisturizing cream heritage, was one of the top brands. Styles had changed. Volume was out and straight and shiny was in.

Napkin models suggest new lines of investigation. I once joined a department that was working from a statistical model that was ten years old. It had been at the heart of a major breakthrough which fueled a huge competitive advantage that doubled the business. But competition had closed the gap in as time passed; they gained directional advantages in the most recent usage study. The statistical model didn't change when the program was run on the data. But there were indications that the model didn't explain the results as well as it had in research run a decade earlier.

Consumer needs were investigated with the universal problem exercise and a constant sum game. This provided the basis for drafting an experience based model. The heritage questionnaire was missing important elements of the model, particularly in the area of perceived failure and performance under stress.

In qualitative research, there were a small faction of consumers that frequently experienced failure. They were always trying new products and had well above average consumption. They seemed important, and were a group that hadn't been identified quantitative research.

The standard questionnaire was overhauled for the next usage test and a new habits and practices study was fielded. The home use test produced a dramatically different, and more predictive statistical model. More than ten of the new direct questions were more influential on the Overall rating than any of the old questions. Failure became a key part of the behavioral segmentation formed from the Habits and Practices data, and failure prone consumers a significant segment.

The Natures of Change

Cheryl

Let's imagine Cheryl, a typical high school teenager. She worries about acne, so she uses Proactiv to get rid of impurities and excess oils. Proactiv divests her skin of pimples.

To get the look she wants for her hair, she buys CHI Salon products. Cheryl can't just use anything since she has fine hair. It takes the combination of several products to acquire the volume that satisfies her.

She is particular about the clothes she wears to school. Her mom bought her bargains off the clearance rack at Walmart, so girls made fun of the way she dressed. Now she shops at the mall with her friends and buys brand names that they all wear.

Cheryl wears five silver bangles on her left wrist. She gets a lot of compliments about them, which makes her feel good. It's a signature flourish of style that, in a small way, elevates her above everybody else.

****

Change Experiences

Big Ideas bring change to our lives. Change comes through four core experiences. Experiences can elevate us above the crowd, helping us to stand apart from everyone else. Other experiences help us fit in and become closer to a community. There are experiences in which we acquire what we need to fulfill our aspirations and desires. Experiences may also free us from something unwanted.

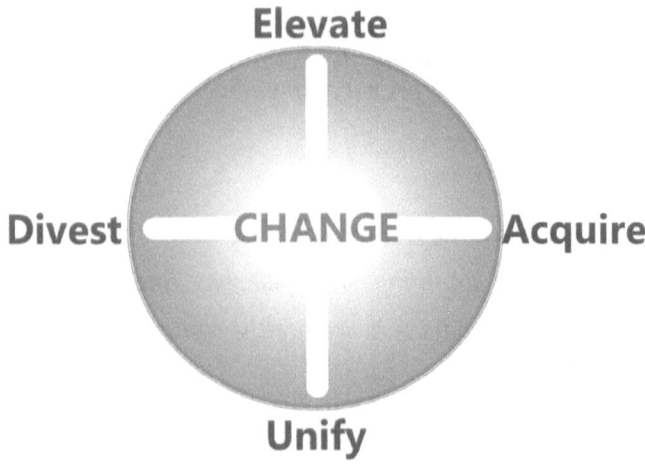

Making Meaning (Diller, Shedroff, Rhea) defines an experience as the sensation of change. Experiencing something requires the recognition of an alteration to our environment, bodies, mind, spirit or any other aspect of ourselves that can sense change. An experience is any process that we have awareness and involvement as it happens.

They define meaning as the sense we make of reality. Assigning meaning to experience is how each of us creates our personal story, value and purpose. We may want economic value, status, identity and emotional connection. But we want them within the overall meaning or set of meanings that are exactly right for us.

Making Meaning differentiates between values and meaning. Values involve preferences. The represent our choices between opposing modes of behavior, and they are shaped not only by ourselves, but also by those around us. For example, let's also say that Cheryl has become a vegetarian because she believes it's the best mode of eating for her health, and she believes in animal rights. These beliefs express a value.

But practicing vegetarianism serves her sense of oneness and community with her friends who are also vegan. And maybe truth, which is meaning.

It's not enough to deliver change; the experience matters too. Are consumers trying to get rid of something, or add something? Do they want to be raised above their peers, or are they trying to join them?

Complimentary Experiences

A complimentary experience reinforces the solving of a functional problem by also satisfying the associated emotional needs. A Big Idea must do more than meet a Need; it must express the right experience too. Sometimes this is incorporated in the execution, but it is mostly embedded in the Big Idea itself. Knowing a Need's complimentary experience will help you recognize a Big Idea. Some call these emotional benefits.

Making Meaning lists fifteen meaningful experiences, which have been mapped on the Change model on the next page:

- **Wonder** – Awe in the presence of a something beyond understanding.

- **Creation** – Producing anything new and original, and having made a lasting contribution in doing so.

- **Beauty** – Gives pleasure to the spirit.

- **Validation** – Feeling valued and worthy of respect.

- **Accomplishment** – A sense of achieving goals and making something of yourself.

- **Duty** – Committing to a cause or responsibility.

- **Justice** – The establishment and assurance of equality and fairness.

- **Harmony** – The balanced and pleasing relationship of parts to a whole in nature, society or individual.

- **Oneness** – A sense of unity with everything around us.

- **Community** - A sense of unity with others around us and connection with other human beings.

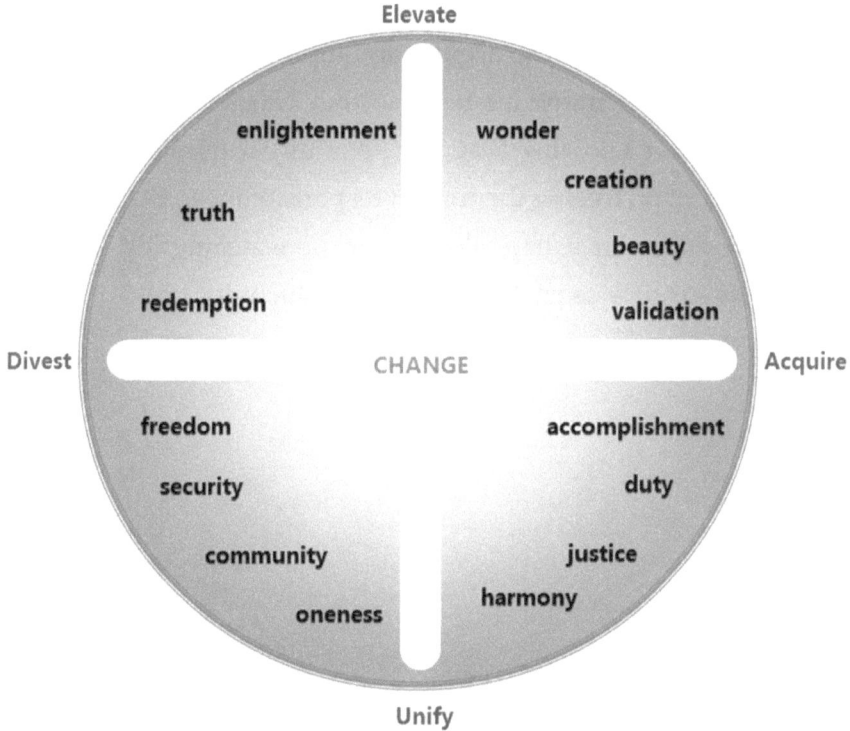

- **Security –** Freedom from worry about loss.

- **Freedom –** Living without unwanted constraints.

- **Redemption -** Atonement or rescue from past failures mistakes or decline.

- **Truth –** Commitment to honesty and integrity.

- **Enlightenment –** Clear understanding through logic or inspiration.

Recall the instant gratification trend discussed in the last chapter. People choose to be busy to acquire accomplishments. People want to save time doing mundane tasks so they can do more important things. Without knowing that, someone might pursue a Big Idea about divestment, freeing them from responsibilities. Except saving time to be spent on a nap, sleeping in or watching TV does not resonate as strongly as enabling higher productivity.

THE NEXT LEVEL

To this point, the aim of this book has been to surface Naked Truths, the shaping undercurrents in your space. Now the work levels up to apply the Truths that you have found.   They are the foundational stimulus for Big Idea generation.

So, ask yourself, how do you feel about the Naked Truths you have? Do you feel you have strong articulations of the Needs, Issues and Forces in the space? If you feel you have deep understanding across all three, then you are ready to find Ties that unite them.

Tying

A "Tie" is a common link between a Need, a Remedy and a Force. It's normally captured in a word or a phrase. A Tie is not a Big Idea. It's a raw notion that can stimulate one.

Think of a Tie as a good fishing spot. It's a place to cast your line because it's where three different undercurrents cross in your space. Ideas that you find there will inherently address Consumer Needs, Remedies, and critical Forces in the marketplace. Ideas that do that are much more likely to be big ones for your business.

Finding Ties is straightforward. Make sets of three Naked Truths that are related in some way, using one from each bucket. Make as many matches as you can. If you start with fifteen Naked Truths in each bucket, you should be able to make at least eight to ten complete connections. It's alright to repeat a Naked Truth in more than one set.

There may be a Naked Truth that seems very powerful by itself, but if it doesn't connect to anything in the other buckets, it's a dead end.

If it's only missing a link to one of the buckets, it's still going to be dead end. However, you may want to revisit that bucket to consider any missing Truths.

A Tie expresses how a complete set of Naked Truths are linked. Examine the complete connections and name them. Keep it short... three words or less if you can.

Tying is best done with a group that brings diversity in thinking and experience. Give your team the three buckets of Truths and ask them to pick ones that inspire them most. Have everyone share a pick. It doesn't matter which bucket the Truth comes from, and it definitely doesn't matter which bucket wins. This exercise insures that everyone reads and internalizes all of them.

You may be tempted to kick off Tying with a PowerPoint deck of background information to educate the participants on the critical information about the project. First consider this Naked Truth about business communication:

> *PowerPoint decks are commonly shown to relay critical information to team members. However, it seems like people remember less than 10% of what is shared, so they tend to default to what they knew before they entered the room.*

If your Naked Truths are well written, background slides are superfluous. They should contain all the relevant stimulus information. It's fine to review the goals for the day, an overview of the Big Idea program and a few details about the hard work that preceded the meeting. But any more than that is unnecessary. In fact, it can be counterproductive. It robs time from the agenda, saps energy from the room and invites fruitless discussion that won't move the team any closer toward accomplishing the objectives of the day.

Ask everyone on the team to work either alone or in a pair to find complete connections. Working in groups of three or more tends to leave somebody on the sideline.

Connections will surely be repeated when the group is divided into individuals or working pairs. But the name of the Tie may not be redundant. It's ideal to converge to a set of eight to twelve titles at minimum, but no more than the number of attendees in the room. To pick which Ties to bring forward, ask the group vote on the titles that are most inspiring, that are most likely to lead to a Big Idea. Ask them to ignore the Naked Truths that hatched them, only considering Ties by themselves.

Case Study – Part 3

Jack reviewed his Need Truths and noted that there were four triggers to consume candy. We eat confections when we are hungry, tired, stressed or bored. It can serve as bridge between meals when we have hunger pangs. Sweets are also a boost of energy when we feel tired, or are about to do something that will make us tired.

The reasons to consume candy while being stressed or bored were not obvious to him. So, he Googled it and found literature that suggested that the goal was the same… to escape the moment. In a way, he thought, candy always provided an escape, either from physical states of hunger and exhaustion or in changing our emotions from a negative state to a positive one. He drew a chocolate bar:

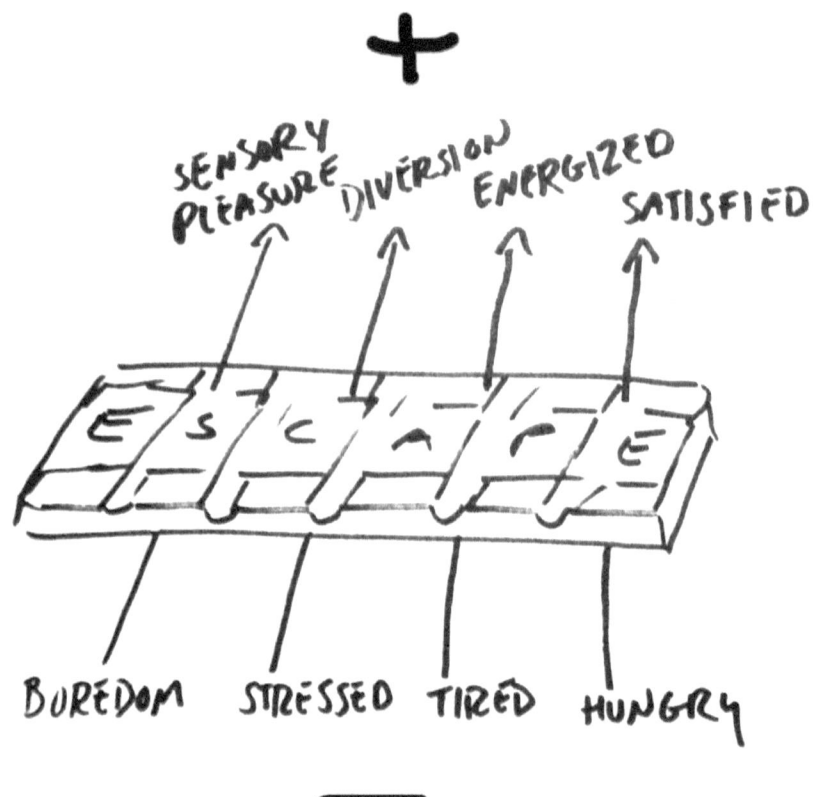

The model revealed a new Need Truth:

> *I eat candy because I am bored, tired, hungry or stressed. It always helps me escape from and undesirable physical state or emotion. But it's only temporary, even momentary.*

Jack sorted his Naked Truths and discovered he had only a few Remedies. That's when he realized he hadn't talked to the scientists at Big Food about opportunities in candy. Over the next few days he met over coffee with various experts and expanded his portfolio of Remedies.

Sugar Substitutes are rarely found in candy because they don't provide the same chemical structure, so diet candy usually has different mouth feel. A structure substitute is necessary to duplicate the texture when sugar is not used.

Diet candy tries to mimic regular candy, but it doesn't because it has a different texture without sugar. Instead of trying to make sugar free candy something that it's not, let it be itself, like Mentos or Icebreaker mints which have their own unique mouth feel.

Caffeine in chocolate is a myth; it contains a similar compound called theobromine that has milder stimulating effects. Caffeine may be a welcome additive to chocolate for those seeking a jolt of energy.

Athletes can benefit from sustained delivery of nutrients and minerals during training, but sports drinks are consumed at breaks. A chew or lozenge could provide a better delivery system.

The more that Jack learned, the more questions he had. He accepted that he could never know everything about candy, but he thought he had gathered enough insight for a Big Idea. He reserved a conference room and invited a few of his coworkers for pizza.

They sorted through the Naked Truths, combined matching sets, and named the Ties. Here is an example of one of the Ties.

Tie: *Organic*
Need: *Limiting the amount of candy my kids eat is one way that I show I love them. I search for heathy alternatives that they like, but are good for them.*
Force: *In today's grocery, the organic section is a store within a store. There is a limited selection of candy now, like chocolate covered organic dried fruit, so could there be an opportunity for other forms of organic candy.*
Remedy: *Modern candy is made with a lot of ingredients, some of which is highly processed and artificial. Modern manufacturing techniques and the cost and availability of raw materials demand it. Acme makes old fashioned styled candy in small batches that is simply made with natural ingredients.*

The meeting produced about a dozen Ties. Jack was feeling comfortable about the directions that were taking shape:

Caffeinated
Organic
Competitive Edge
Meal Bridge

Simple Ingredients

Energy

Low Cal

Destressing

Healthy Kids

Organic Escape

Chocoholic Pleasures

Fortified

Sports

4: IMAGINE

"Imagination is everything. It is the preview of life's coming attractions."

- Albert Einstein

Creativity solves problems, but imagination conceives alternative systems, realities and worlds. It envisions a destination to change the game and drive innovation.

Imagination benefits from linear, radiant and heuristic thinking. Edward De Bono described linear thinking as "vertical thinking", using reasoning to form a step by step process to solve a problem. It is logical and realistic.

Radiant thinking has been described as lateral, horizontal or thinking sideways. It finds a new and original ways to look at a problem that may not be logical. It looks for tangents, alternatives, analogies and parallels. Radiant is the most accurate adjective since it infers that thoughts move in any direction. It is creative and boundless.

My friend and I have thinking styles that are polar opposite. She is a linear thinker while I am a radiant thinker, so we can clash when we work together. When we encounter a problem, she formulates a plan to solve it. It annoys her when I don't see the next step (which is obvious to her), or am still thinking of other approaches. I get frustrated that she has jumped to action without thinking about other ways to go about it. When she is faced with a problem she thinks in terms of step one, two, three, etc. I think of trying A, B, C, D, etc. We work best when we discuss all our thoughts to get the right solution and plan.

Heuristic thinking extracts rules of thumb and shortcuts. It comes through experience and helps to reason through challenges. It employs the process of elimination, or trial and error. Remember math problems in middle school that started with a phrase like, "two trains traveling toward each other…" Most would read the entire paragraph and take notes before getting to the last sentence which stated the question to be answered. Heuristic thinkers know from prior quizzes that the last sentence is always the question to be answered, and read that first. Then they skim the rest of the paragraph to extract only the relevant information. If asked to calculate 18 X 9, a heuristic approach could be multiplying 18 X 10 and then subtract 18 to come up with the answer of 162. It's clever and unconventional.

This chapter discusses the five kinds of Big Ideas and story archetypes. But first it introduces strategic imagination as a prerequisite to focus ideation.

Strategic Imagination

"Imagination governs the world."

- Napoleon Bonaparte

An abundance of Big Idea candidates will emerge out of this process. The criteria for choosing which one, or which one to do first, should be based on the strategic fit with your business. Many companies struggle to form actionable innovation strategies. Here are eight "Toos" that victimize strategies.

- **Too Abstract:** Stating principles and beliefs can make an organization feel good about the company, but lack a call to action.

- **Too Tactical:** An Innovation strategy is not a master plan. It should never be an exercise of reverse engineering to fit the initiatives that are currently resourced.

- **Too Narrow:** Drawing boundaries that aren't necessary can quash innovation. One pitfall is to limit spaces to what the company does today verses what it can do tomorrow.

- **Too Optimistic:** The time, effort and resources to deliver an innovation can be underestimated. It's also common to overestimate how much stakeholders can be influenced.

"Behind every big failure is a big ego."

- **Too Competitive:** A focus on competition can result in short term gains, but long-term innovation can suffer.

- **Too Much Internal Focus:** Consumer needs can be forgotten when an innovation program is aimed at cutting costs and increasing productivity.

- **Too Numbered:** Let measures be measures, not the goals. Innovation strategy should not be expressed in financial terms. Reserve numbers to measure success.

- **Too Many:** An innovation strategy with a long list of priorities has no priorities.

Strategy Questions

This is a good point in the Big Idea journey to flesh out critical business strategies. These five questions help the organization ground itself in reality and consumer needs in an inspirational way. Alternatively, they can be valuable team exercise *before* setting sail on a Big Idea program.

Who are you?

Assess the strengths of the business by honestly critiquing what it has done in the past. Then embrace them as keys to the future. Go beyond knowing its abilities, know the neighborhood… the landscape, your neighbor's skills (customers and competitors) and what's around the corner.

> *"Look well into* **thyself***; there is sources of strength which will always spring up if thou wilt always look."*

> - *Marcus Aurelius*

Why do you exist?

Articulation of an actionable purpose is crucial to creating a vision for your business. A purpose must be achievable and measurable in consumer terms, connecting to functional and emotional consumer needs that are not met by today's solutions. Ask, how can you be a champion for your consumers?

What must be defeated?

Look into your consumers' world to identify what keeps them from obtaining your stated purpose today. Think of these as your enemies, rather than your competition.

Make a list of problems and barriers that consumers are facing. Every problem is a battle that could be fought, too many to undertake. So, look for themes in the list of battles. Grouping battles under a theme constitutes a war that can be waged. Choose the war that 1) will have the most impact on consumers, and 2) has the most value to your business. It will be tempting to choose several wars, but that will only be possible if there are sufficient resources and capacity to sign up for all of them.

War is deliberately chosen as a metaphor to underscore that an innovation strategy is a call to action. There must be urgency and commitment to defeat the enemies of the consumer. However, other language might be more appropriate for your team. Instead of battles, you can describe them as barriers to overcome, mountains to climb, puzzles to solve or chains to break. Instead of wars, you can call them missions to undertake.

"Reality can be beaten with enough imagination."

- Mark Twain

Where are you going?

A mission profits from a destination that will indicate when the war has been won. Continuing to innovate on a benefit that is well met will not be as valuable to the business as it would be to venture into a new war. Imagine how consumer's lives will be different and the possibilities that will emerge when the purpose is fulfilled. It should inspire and direct design, marketing and product development.

Fill in the blank:

We won't rest until _____

How will you get there?

Wars are fought with armies and resources. Brainstorm organization changes that would improve the chances for success and accelerate progress. Identify potential partners and external resources that could be allies.

Outline a master plan that sequences the battles to be fought in the war. Put the short term, easy wins first, the battles that require time and investment last.

> *"You have to pick your battles wisely. Not every conflict is worth turning into a major battle."*

> *- Sun Tzu*

Big Ideas

If Ties are fishing spots, then Big Ideas are the fish. There are five different kinds. A single Tie is unlikely to stimulate every type, but you may surprise yourself if you try.

Big Ideas are compelling, central organizing thoughts that will drive and shape all aspects of design and communication. Big Ideas are simple and explain themselves. They are unforgettable and bring a new frame of reference so the product/service won't be viewed in the same way again, changing what matters. They connect to a Naked Truth about consumer needs in a meaningful way. They are a promise to consumers and set clear and inspirational goals for innovation. Here are the types:

Providence
This is a credential, certification or approval that matters to consumers. It can also be about how it's made, what is in it, or where it's made.

The American Dental Association Seal was another Big Idea for Crest. The brand was launched in 1956 with moderate success. In 1960, Crest was the first to secure an approval from dentists. It was no small feat, as toothpaste wasn't considered necessary by the professional organization at the time. It was merely providing good taste as an enticement to foster regular brushing habits.

Announcement of the endorsement was big news. Wall Street temporarily suspended trading on Procter and Gamble stock that day. Crest became the leading brand by 1962. The ADA endorsement has been an important element of their business strategy ever since. Crest still provides free samples to the dentists' patients and has sought and obtained approval for every new toothpaste that they've introduced.

Liquid foundation make-up was a dominant form in the 1990s. Bare Escentuals was a small company that made a dry make-up line. They found a Big Idea in mineral based make-up. The line was renamed "Bare Minerals" and it entered the infomercial universe. Spokeswomen persuasively argued that liquid foundation seeped into pores and gave you pimples. Bare Mineral formulas were dry and had natural pigments, so they were inherently better for your skin, felt better and gave a natural look. The company grew from six stores to 120 company-owned shops, 880 beauty product and online retailers, and 1,500 spas and salons.

To Generate Providence Big Ideas

- Identify any specifications or requirements for your innovation that can be related back to any of the Ties.

  - Write a recipe for your product. Include the ingredients and how it's made. Find connections to Ties.

  - Generate a list of whose opinions, certifications or approvals would matter to consumers.

Evidence

It's a moment that demonstrates the advantages of the innovation. It can be plucked from the consumers' real life or be a plausible situation that consumers know to be true. The details of the event can be exaggerated, as long the portrayal of the innovation is honest. It can incorporate yardsticks, milestones and personal goals.

Wendy's "where's the beef?" campaign was an Evidence Big Idea launched in 1984. Wendy's had 10% larger burgers than other fast food chains, but had failed to grow the business with that message. The iconic commercial portrays a moment in which three elderly ladies walk up to a counter and stand under a sign that says, "Home of the Big Bun". Then they lean over to inspect a burger on a plate. One of them lifts off the top bun to expose a tiny burger not much bigger than the pickle. Clara Peller utters the phrase that made her a celebrity, "where's the beef?" Although the details of the scene are exaggerated for humorous effect, it references familiar moments: ordering at a stainless-steel counter and opening the sandwich to examine the food. Feeling cheated was the emotional stress that was dramatized. No numerical claims were included, only that Wendy's has more beef than the leading chain.

Crest Tartar Control was launched in 1990 to bring a new benefit to oral care. Before its introduction, preventing tartar didn't excite consumers. They didn't care because tartar didn't threaten the health of their teeth and was regularly removed at dentist visits. Crest made tartar prevention relevant by claiming that its new paste made dentist visits easier. Anxiety about teeth cleaning is common; it's uncomfortable and a new cavity can make one feel inadequate or guilty. The moment that was dramatized was the end of an easy, problem-free visit.

To Generate Evidence Big Ideas

- Imagine situations where the benefits of your innovation would be either most obvious or most important. Picture moments… snapshots or video clips.

- Do kitchen experiments to demonstrate Ties. Use materials around your home, the craft shop or hardware store to prove advantages of your product to yourself. Modify to experiments in various ways to accentuate any differences that you observe.

Specialization

The innovation satisfies the demands of special people, conditions or tasks which consumers believe are relevant to them. It becomes a Big Idea when the product has crossover appeal, being used for lesser purposes than its stated intention.

Yoga pants are flexible and form-fitting garments that were designed for yoga and other activities that involve a lot of movement, bending and stretching. Comfort and easy care makes them popular for casual wear; so much so that they are worn less often for athletic activities.

SUVs (Sports Utility Vehicles) were designed to be driven on and off the road. They have higher road clearances, sturdy truck-like frames and four-wheel drive. But their interiors are more comfortable and have smoother rides than trucks. The Jeep Cherokee was the first modern SUV, although there have been many forerunners. It offered parents a cooler, tougher looking alternative to minivans. Very few drivers take them off road, unless you count cul de sacs.

To Generate Specialization Big Ideas

- Imagine what person, situation, activity or thing would be a torture test for the Tie. Think of extremes. If the innovation can work for that, then it might be good for almost anyone or anything.

- Use torture tests that you imagine to stimulate ideas for Providence and Evidence.

Transformation

Describe the results using a metaphor or analogy that has value to people. It tells the consumer how they will be changed by using the innovation.

Vidal Sassoon gained notoriety for his bob-cut hairstyle which became popular with fashion designers and

Hollywood actresses in the late 1960s and 1970s. He capitalized on his fame by launching his own line of hair products. Few women could afford to visit one of his exclusive salons, but anyone could buy his shampoo. His assortment promised professional results at home. Today, that Big Idea is the basis for most brands in the super premium tier of hair products sold in the mass market.

Snickers launched its "you're not you when you're hungry" campaign in 2010. It's flips the Transformation type. Celebrities personify moods and behaviors of famished people. Betty White (weakness), Aretha Franklin (diva), Rosanne Barr (cranky), Robin Williams (loopy) and even Godzilla (anger) have appeared in the popular spots. One bite of a Snickers bar transformed them back into themselves.

To Generate Transformation Big Ideas

- List the standards of excellence related to the Ties, both inside and outside of the innovation space.

- Google images for Ties, using the visuals to stimulate new thoughts.

Mimic

The innovation manifests itself as an intuitive, appealing metaphor or analogy. It is like Transformation, except that the metaphor expresses the attributes of the product rather than the results.

Slim Fast is a diet meal replacement drink that mimics a milk shake, which is an indulgence that would otherwise be off the menu for weight watchers. Pampers Swaddlers is an infant diaper that wraps and feels like a swaddling blanket. Under Armour began as compression t-shirts for professional teams. The branding is a metaphor that expresses strength and protection, which is appealing in competitive sports. It is also consistent with the brand promise, since soggy cotton underwear can be distracting, which is ultimately a weakness. The technical benefit of the fabric is to wick away moisture for a drier, lighter feel.

To Generate Mimic Big Ideas

- Use the output of the transformation exercise to find analogies for the innovation.

- How is the product like a service, or how is the service like a product?

- Imagine your innovation is a child. What would be its hero? What are its parents and other relatives?

- If the innovation went to a masquerade ball as its alter ego, what costume would it wear?

Innovation Archetypes

Archetypes were discussed in Chapter 2. Personality archetypes are seen in brand characters. Realm archetypes form real estate for market segments. Innovation narratives also have archetypes; story lines that are repeated across various goods and services. These examples may incite creativity if you get stuck trying to ideate any type of Big Idea.

- A **Mash Up** is the mixing of at least two distinctly separate things to make something better. Chobani Flip combines yogurt with various crunchy mixes to create snacks that resemble deserts.

- **Building a better mousetrap** involves a genius who solves an old problem by changing a paradigm. James Dyson reimagined vacuums with "cyclonic action" so that they never lose suction.

- **Reframing** brings new facts to the table to open new points of view. Arm & Hammer exploited a benefit of baking soda that wasn't well known, that it absorbed odors. Today open boxes can be found in millions of refrigerators. Tide Coldwater revealed that it cost $0.50 to heat a hot water load, giving people more reason to run cold water loads.

- **Democratization** makes expensive or exclusive goods and services available to everyone. Tang is a breakfast drink mix that astronauts took on space flights.

- 3M was developing a new super adhesive. One formula didn't work very well at all, but a scientist observed that it could stick paper to surfaces and be peeled off without damage. He put the glue on the back of paper squares and posted notes around the lab. That was the first prototype for Post-it notes. It was a **fortunate accident**.

- Some innovation is an **exaggeration** of the ordinary. Callaway's Big Bertha spawned an oversized golf club segment.

- **Necessity is the mother of invention**. Players on the University of Florida's football team were wilting in the summer heat. An assistant coach met with UF researchers to find an antidote. They concocted a beverage with a balance of carbohydrates and electrolytes that they called "Gatorade."

- **Doing it backwards** breaks conventional wisdom to produce a breakthrough alternative. The Atkins diet has a meat laden menu, which is counterintuitive for weight loss.

- Making an **unexpected connection** is another common innovation story. George de Mestral found burs on his clothes after taking a walk outdoors. It was his inspiration for Velcro.

- An **enlightened point of view** can be the source of socially concerned innovation and new experiences. Chipotle Mexican Grills serve "food with integrity" and a dining experience unlike any other fast food restaurant.

- The **exception becomes the rule**. 60 minutes, the popular TV news magazine, broadcast a special interest story about a small village in Russia that had exceptionally long life spans. It was reported that yogurt was an important part of their diet. This inspired a successful campaign for Dannon that popularized yogurt with Americans.

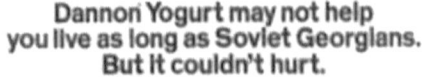

- An **endless quest for perfection** yields extraordinary innovation. Two Detroit scientists wanted to create a superior surface cleaner, and on the 409th try, they did.

Case Study – Part 4

Jack invited employees from both Acme and Big Food to brainstorm Big Ideas. He briefly exposed the group to the Ties that his informal team had generated over lunch, but he let the new joint team build a set from scratch. It was one of the highlights of the day because Acme and Big Food employees were paired up and got to know one another.

After the group decided on the most promising Ties, they split back up into their pairs to think of Big Ideas for them. Some of the Ties were easier than others, since some of the Ties, like "Chocoholic Pleasures" were actually Big Ideas already. Others elicited concern, like Microbrewery and Margarita Ville, as they referenced alcohol. But the pairs that generated them were passionate about their potential.

Here were some of the Big Ideas that were generated:

Red Bull Candy

Certified Organic

Fourth Quarter Energy

Carob Delights

Candy Salsa

Greetings from Margarita Ville

Sport

Snackables (Like Lunchables)

Daily Requirement

Chocolight

Delights of Eden

Microbrewery

Fitness Chews

5: REALIZE

Now that you have some Big Ideas, explore their implications and where innovation would lead. Don't test Big Ideas (and Naked Truths) with consumers. Consumers may find them off-putting in their raw form.

JK Rowling wrote a series of preadolescent books about boy and his friends attending a school of magic. The boy was the only one who could thwart an evil wizard's plan to rule the world. Had the publisher pitched the idea to focus groups, Harry Potter may never have seen print. It hardly seemed like suitable subject matter for children.

So, bring Big Ideas to life with the tools in this Chapter and explore the output in research. Be prepared to for major iterative refinement with consumers.

Imagination Boards

Fishing Trip

A father took his three boys fishing for the first time. "Watch how I cast," he said as he baited his hook. He flipped his line into the river and got a bite in less than a minute. He reeled in a fish and proudly presented it to his gawking children. "Now you try," he said.

The boys stared at him blankly while holding their junior fishing poles. "What's the matter?" He asked. But they were silent. "Do you have any questions?"

The first boy asked, "What's casting like?"

"It's like tossing a ball. Think of your pole as extension of your arm and the bait as the ball." His father smiled.

"Now I understand." The first son said. And his father thought he might grow up to be a designer.

"Not me," the second son said. "How does it work?"

His father kneeled on one knee and explained the parts of the rod. He showed him the spool of line, the hooks, the bob and the lead weight. The he showed him how to straighten his finger at just the right moment to release the nylon fishing line.

"Now I understand." The second son said. His dad suspected he would grow up to be an engineer or a scientist.

"I get all that," the third son said. *But I still want to know what works."*

"What works?" The father asked

"For bait."

"Some hook live worms; some make feather lures. I've even seen people soak hot dog chunks in Kool- Aid. It depends on what you are trying to catch. I usually experiment to find the best bait. Sometimes I learn from other fishermen too."

"Now I understand." The third boy said. And his father could see that he might be a business man when he grew up.

The boys fished all morning and filled their pails full of fish.

****

Imagination boards start to paint a tangible vision of what Big Ideas will become if pursued. They explode each Big Idea with a horde of tactical seed ideas that help bring it to life for everyone. Use Imagination Boards as a Concept Brief. They also can be used to inform Design, R&D and other functions.

An Imagination Board includes:

- The Big Idea.

- A definition of the target consumer.

- The look, tone, feel and ultimately the emotional experience of the product or service.

- The vocabulary (words, phrases, images and idioms) associated with the Big Idea. Create a code for the Big Idea. For example, let's say it's "Industrial Strength". Examine a variety of Industrial Strength products to identify the common language of words, design elements and visualizations. Translate them to fit your innovation.

- Seed ideas for claims, benefits, demos and other visualization. Include specific thoughts for products or services that could be offered. In other words, ideas for what would be said, shown and sold.

- The Naked Truths that are connected to the Big Idea.

A template is found on the next page. Examples of imagination boards appear in Part 3 of the case study.

Big Idea:

Seed claims

benefits

sensorial attributes

demo ideas

visualizations and various product ideas

Target:

Need Naked Truth:

Remedy Naked Truth:

Force Naked Truth:

Non-Cognitive Expression

Big Ideas are often provocative. Therefore, they may be best expressed non-cognitively, particularly those that are metaphorical. Your imagination board will give you the means to express your Big Idea without actually saying your Big Idea.

At one time, I was working on a new sensorial hair care line. One of the Big Ideas was "addiction." Early concepts featured the word to describe the attributes of the collection. They bombed in qualitative research. Consumers said they didn't want to be addicted to anything.

The concept evolved and stopped calling addiction by name, but still had phrases that could be used to describe it:

- Hair you can't keep your fingers away from.

- Decadent lather.

- Get lost in exotic essences.

- So good, you can't get enough.

- You can't wait for your next shower.

Consumers were drawn to the subtle approach. Some said, "ooooo... that's sounds addictive!" Implying the addictive nature of the products made it one of our most appealing concepts.

Computers were gray, boxy and ugly in 1998. The internet was futuristic and not fully understood by most consumers, but they liked what they could find online. Apple designed the original Indigo iMac to meet the growing popularity of the internet and demands for speed and memory, with the simplicity of Macintosh operating systems. The underlying Big Idea was "alien technology." Steve Jobs said in the launch event that, "it looks like it came from another planet." This was the closest Apple ever came to stating the Big Idea transparently. (It's entirely possible that they were oblivious to it.) The monitor was shaped like E.T.'s head. It glowed like the space ship in "Close Encounters of the Third Kind". Beyond appearances, it featured highly advanced technology. The floppy disc drive was missing because it was becoming obsolete. Instead, it made USB ports standard. It was superfast with a big screen and lots of memory compared to competition. Apple didn't have to say the words alien technology, since everything about it said alien technology.

Prototyping

Prototypes help make Big Ideas concrete and uncover flaws. There was once a major brand that wanted to revamp its architecture. SKUs had proliferated through years of new product initiatives. Consumers complained that the store shelf was confusing and that it was hard to find what they wanted.

The team came up with several potential Big Ideas to inspire a new line up that would transform the brand and make the shelf more shoppable. There were many ideas for new exciting products to replace the current range. However, when SKUs were totaled for each of the architecture candidates, it was always far less than the number of SKUs that were already on the shelf. Fewer SKUs would mean fewer sales and a smaller business.

The team labored to find an acceptable architecture that would maintain the current size of the shelf. Each new Big Idea was prototyped by writing all potential SKUs on post-its to stick on a wall. It took weeks until they found a Big Idea that generated a lineup that met the objective.

To start prototyping, ask, **"What would we sell?"** Brainstorm a list of products, options or services and their benefits. Then ask, **"How would it work?"** Investigate what inventions would be required to deliver the vision. Have a discussion with experts about possibilities. It's better to ask a technologist *how* something can be done rather than *if* something can be done. If the first answer is no, then understand why and the assumptions being made. Probe for an alternative and how close it could come to delivering the ideal. Remove implausible product ideas from your list, or modify them so they are realistic.

Make "works-like" prototypes if appropriate. "Works-like" doesn't have to be made of the same materials or resemble the final product; its intent is only to explore how it would act and whether the problem is solvable using that approach. Ideas that sound feasible may not be when prototyped.

Create "looks-like" prototypes. It may be as simple as writing out the options being considered, as it was with the architecture project. Drawings can be instructive. There are times when three-dimensional prototypes are worthwhile, especially if user interactions should be evaluated. Modeling clay, craft supplies, and bits and pieces of other packaging and products can be fashioned into physical representations for handling. Looks-like prototyping can be explored and tested with consumers.

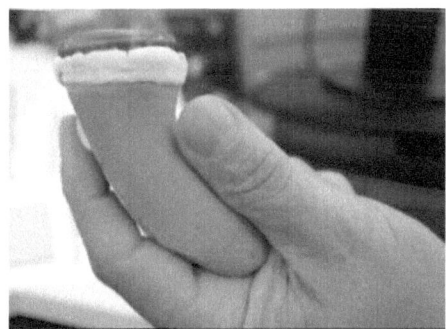

Names & Claims

The Big Idea should inspire potential claims for communication with consumers. A claim should be no more than eight to ten words. It must make a meaningful promise, normally one that must be proven with facts and data.

Names may also play a key role in messaging. However, there is a tendency to place too much importance on finding the right brand name. A name with positive natural associations can be advantageous in the launch of a new brand. But over time the name will take on the experiences the brand delivers as its identity. eBay and Amazon have strong names, but the power is not in the names themselves. The founder of eBay wanted to trademark his parent company's name for his website. However, Echo Bay wasn't available for a website, so he went with an abbreviation instead. Amazon was partly chosen because search engines of the time listed websites alphabetically.

Trademarks are a crowded territory, so don't fall in love with a name before it's been cleared. I recall doing qualitative research on more than hundred name candidates and finding that the ten most appealing were already taken. It took months to hit on an unblocked option. It wasn't anyone's favorite and had limited relevance for communication, but it was proprietary.

On the other hand, the name of an individual "version" can be critical if it must function as the primary communication. Brands can offer too many products to advertise them separately. So, the version name may be the first and only information that consumers receive.

Version names should:

- **Direct consumers to the product(s) which will satisfy them best.** Offering variants enables a brand to deliver higher satisfaction with specializations that address a spectrum of varied consumer needs or desires. The primary function of a name is to direct consumers to the right variant for them. It's best that name transparently communicate the job that the product is designed to do and the key benefit.

- **Have appeal.** A name should be eye catching so consumers pick that product over the competition.

- **Differentiate from each other.** Version names should have a distinct place in the range of products or services. Products that appear to have a similar purpose create confusion at the shelf. Redundancy is also not an efficient use of space.

It is serendipitous if the name can be trademarked or reinforces the brand voice/character. Otherwise, those factors should only be considered as tiebreakers for two equally appealing and descriptive options.

A thesaurus is your best resource for generating names. Your Imagination Board may help you make connections as well as spark Google searches, particularly for images.

Explore potential claims or names with consumers in one-on-ones qualitative research using a sorting exercise. An effective technique is to print claims on index cards and ask people to sort them into piles. First, ask them to make two piles, one for those liked more and the other for those liked less. Next, take the favorite pile and divide them again, into more and less. Then have them pick their three most favorite and rank them. After selections are made, ask about their reasoning. Probing can be done on specific statements from any pile, liked and disliked. This exercise can accommodate as many as a hundred different statements or names.

If the innovation is outside of consumer experience, then explore names and claims with "Billboards". A Billboard contains a visual of the product and may be essential to make stronger claims believable. Images should be kept simple. Ideally, one image should be employed for all the claims and names being explored.

Chipotle has run an effective billboard campaign about their burritos, pairing a claim with a simple visual. They are an approximate blueprint for creating your own billboards for sorting research.

Case Study – Part 5

After getting feedback from the other attendees, pairs created Imagination Boards. Some of the Big Ideas evolved and changed. Magazines were torn to get some images; the internet was the source of others. There would be too many to describe here, but a few notable ones are on the pages that follow.

"Sweet Berries" was one of the Big Ideas that changed while composing an Imagination Board. Its original name was "Candy Salsa". The pair observed similarities between the look, tone and feel of the candy dish images and berry photos that they found. Their intention was to make candy that mimicked real berries… juicy, flavorful, good for you and completely natural. Unlike fruit roll-ups that were dry and chewy, these berry sized candies would burst in your mouth. Some would be filled with juice or cream.

"Fitness Chews" targeted active women. Sports drinks and nutrition brands appeared aimed to men, so the pair suspected it could be a unique positioning. They conceived of a new Naked Truth… that someone trying to stay on fitness regimen would have less energy if they were on a diet. They envisioned sealable pouches of fortified, reduced sugar dark chocolate rounds that were infused with vitamins, electrolytes and caffeine. Fitness Chews rose out of the "Sport" Tie and celebrated keeping up with the spinning class instructor.

The group had disliked Microbrewery when they first heard it. Candy was for kids, so some worried about its alcoholic connotations. But the authoring pair was excited about the idea and promised not to make the idea a literal expression.

The idea was a hit when the board was shared. There are many microbrewery-like lines in the carbonated beverage aisle. They have premium images, quality ingredients and taste great. Some focus on old fashioned drinks, while others have very experiential flavors. Acme already was microbrewery for candy in many ways, but lacked the branding. Many Imagination Boards had potential, but Microbrewery was the only one that could be executed with Acme's current recipes, requiring little investment. New flavor experiences could be developed in future.

Jack believed he had found his lead Big Idea, along with a handful of others the Big Food could invest in for the future. His next step was to write a proposal to ask for funds to explore branding for the Microbrewery idea.

Sweet Berries

NATURAL	*GLUTEN FREE*
HEALTHY	*FRUIT CONCENTRATE*
DELICIOUS	*HONEY*
SIMPLE RECIPES	*BERRY JUICE*
WHOLESOME	*JUICY*
NUTRITIOUS	*REAL*
VITAMINS	*LOOKS LIKE CANDY KIDS LOVE*
CAFFEINE FREE	*CHEWS*
FILLED	*CHOCOLATE COVERED*

Target: Mothers with pre-school and school age children.

Limiting the amount of candy my kids eat is one way that I show I love them. I search for healthy alternatives that they like, but are good for them. (Need)

Modern candy is made with a lot of ingredients, some of which is highly processed and artificial. Modern manufacturing techniques and the cost and availability of raw materials demand it. Acme makes old fashioned styled candy in small batches that is simply made with natural ingredients. (Remedy)

In today's grocery, the organic section is a store within a store. There is a limited selection of candy now, like chocolate covered organic dried fruit, so could there be an opportunity for other forms of organic candy. (Force)

Fitness Chews

CHOCOLATE	DESIGNED FOR WOMEN	BOOSTS
METABOLISM	CURBS HUNGER	ENERGY
BURN CALORIES	LOW CALORIE	NUTRIENTS
REPLENISHES	HEALTHY	WHOLESOME
ACTIVATES	CONCENTRATED	BALANCE
SMALL		

Target: Active women 13-50.

I limit my calories because being trim is part of a healthy lifestyle. But it's hard to get fit when your diet leaves you without enough energy to exercise. (Need)

Sports drinks are growing in the soft drink aisle, perhaps because it's viewed as a healthy drink. He wonders how candy can become part of this trend... how can candy meet sports drinks? (Force)

Athletes can benefit from sustained delivery of nutrients and minerals during training, but sports drinks are consumed at breaks. A chew or lozenge could provide a better delivery system. (Remedy)

Microbrewery

SMALL COMPANY	CANE SUGAR
SMALL MATCHES	NATURALLY FLAVORED
LIMITED EDITIONS	FROM FAR AWAY PLACES
OLD FASHIONED RECIPE	UNIQUE EXPERIENCES
FAMILY OWNED	TRADITION
PASSION FOR CANDY	PROUD PERFECTIONISTS
PREMIUM INGREDIENTS	EXPERIMENTAL
NEVER CUT CORNERS	HAND CRAFTED

Target: Men and women ages 30-65.

I eat candy because I am bored, tired, hungry or stressed. It always helps me escape from and undesirable physical state or emotion. But it's only temporary, even momentary. (Need)

Modern candy is made with a lot of ingredients, some of which is highly processed and artificial. Modern manufacturing techniques and the cost and availability of raw materials demand it. Acme makes old fashioned styled candy in small batches that is simply made with natural ingredients. (Remedy)

Soft drinks have non-flavor sub-segments to better meet the functional and dietary needs of their consumers. The candy aisle can evolve in the same way. (Force)

Locking on a Big Idea

Jack's Big Idea was obvious to the team. Sometimes that's enough to make a proposal for starting a project. But most of the time there will be no clear winner after Imagination Boards are finished. Seven characteristics of a Big Idea were introduced in Chapter 1. Leverage them as a pros and cons checklist for the candidates that have been developed.

1) Simple
2) Explains itself
3) Contractual
4) Meaningful
5) Reframes
6) Unforgettable
7) Inspirational

Some of the characteristics have been baked in by the process, but these three attributes deserve further investigation:

- **Meaningful**
  Write concepts for the Big Idea candidates and test them with consumers. Rely on your findings about names and claims to strengthen them. Include the specific products that would be available, along with pricing, if the Big Idea is executed. There are principles and effective techniques for developing concepts, but that's a subject for another book.

- **Contractual**

  Do the Big Ideas make promises that can be kept? To confirm that they do, review claims in the concepts for being supportable. At the same time, there is a difference between what is legally claimable and the actual product experience. So, give the innovation to consumers to confirm that it lives up claims being made in the concept.

  If nothing is ready for consumer feedback, consider a "placebo" study. Give people one of today's solutions, or a placebo, with a concept. It will likely disappoint the users, but talk to them to learn what would have met their expectations. For example, in qualitative research, consumers said they didn't want any suds in with a new product to wash fruit and vegetables. The team arranged a panel in which participants were given a spray bottle of water to wash apples and broccoli at sinks. People were dissatisfied; there was no evidence that the produce was clean. In fact, they requested a little bit of suds as a signal that it was working.

- **Inspirational**

  How do the Big Idea candidates fit with the organization's purpose and vision? Which provides a sustainable and workable platform for launching future innovation? This is a conversation to have with key stakeholders. The best Big Idea for the company may not be the one with the highest scoring concept.

CONCLUDING THOUGHT

This is a proven, systematic approach
that efficiently produces an abundance
of Big Ideas. You may feel that additional
research and investigation is needed, beyond
the techniques and tools that have been prescribed
here. That's great! But shortcuts are not recommended.

Writing Naked Truths, creating Napkin Models and
Imagination boards can be intellectually challenging
and taxing. Doing all of it with excellence
takes discipline. Consider it the
price of success.

The author is available for training
and consultation at:

Rienzo.Paul@Gmail.com

APPENDIX 1:
WORKSHOP DESIGNS

Many activities described in this book can be done with teams. This appendix shares outlines for several workshops.

Consumer Needs Workshop

It should take only one to two hours to generate a host of Naked Truths if the team has a good understanding of the space.

Print the list of Universal Problems onto half sheets of paper. Deal a Problem to each participant. Put unused sheets in the center of the table. Ask everyone to jot down how each Problem is relevant to consumers, based on what they know about them. Write directly on the card.

After writing one down, have them pass their sheet to someone else, or exchange it with an unused card. Continue until the cards are filled.

Debrief the group on what they believe was most critical to the project. Silent ideation is preferable to group brainstorming for this task; thoughts can flow so quickly that it's impossible to keep up with charting, even if there are several scribes. However, you may want to read some out loud if writing slows.

After notes have been made on all the cards, gather consensus about the most relevant problems. Then utilize the "Real/Deal" framework to translate the most relevant Problems into Naked Truths.

Workshops to identify Naked Truths for Remedies and Forces may also be desirable, however the design should be customized meet the challenges of each unique project. In addition to tools described in Chapter 2, Edward De Bono's *Serious Creativity: Using the Power of Lateral Thinking to Create New Ideas* is a good resource for techniques to break assumptions and open minds.

REAL		DEAL
A Desire		
A Fact of Life	*And Why*	*But*
A Habit		
A Personal Value		

Strategy Workshop

Gather your team together for half of a day. You'll need Post-It Notes, chart pads, markers and wall space.

- **Who are you?**
  Brainstorm your core strengths, weaknesses, competitive advantages and disadvantages. What were the most successful innovations (Hall of Famers) and what was behind them? What were the biggest failures and why were they disappointing? After charting a list, ask the group to find patterns and commonalities. Converge to the top three innovation assets of your company.

- **Why do you exist?**
  Brainstorm all the ways that you can be a champion for your consumers. Use Five Whys to break down abstract or subjective thoughts into achievable, measurable terms. Converge to a simple articulation. This is your purpose.

- **What must be defeated?**
  What battles can you to fight to become a champion for your consumers? What mountains could you climb? What chains must be broken?

  Organize battles into groupings of similar issues. Give each group a title that captures the common theme in the battles. The title is a war that can be declared. Agree on the two or three wars that are winnable and would make the biggest impact on the consumer. These are candidates for innovation focus.

- **Where are you going?**

  Generate a list for each war that fills in this blank:

  We won't rest until _____

  The list should only include things that are meaningful to consumers. Use the experiences from the section on the Natures of Change in Chapter 3. Metaphors and analogies can be helpful in describing how the consumers' world will be different after winning the war and achieve your purpose.

- **How will you get there?**

  Pick battles for each war and sequence them as initiatives in a master plan. Imagine the initiatives that will progress you to the destination. Revisit the question of which war is most winnable and would have the biggest impact on the business. This is the first war to fight.

Big Idea Workshop

This outline can be conducted with six to thirty participants. It's designed to produce one Big Idea and Imagination Board for each participant. Create a relaxed, unhurried environment by allowing people to complete tasks without firm time restraints. Schedule ample breaks to make calls and answer emails, but insist that phones and laptops are put away while in session... until computers are required for the final task. Free yourself to coach people through the exercises, particularly when working in pairs.

- **Briefing**
  The introduction should live up to its name, be brief. Show a few slides about the project objectives and the process, including a slide about the five types of Big Ideas. Rely on Naked Truths to convey key project information in the next step.

- **Review Naked Truths**
  Every individual should be given a complete set of Naked Truths. There should be twelve to twenty from each bucket. Ask them to peruse all of them and select the Truth they find inspiring. Share favorites with the group, introducing themselves one at a time.

  It works well to print insights onto label stock so they can be peeled and stuck to chart paper later. Give them a letter or a number for easy reference.

- **Find Ties**

  Pair up to match Needs, Remedies and Forces. Paste sets together on a chart pad sheet. Then title each set by what Ties them together. Once pairs have finished, have individuals browse others' work, marking favorites with a pen or sticker. Tell them to focus exclusively on the Ties and not the Truths. It's a good idea to limit the number of Ties that they can pick.

- **Visualize**

  Have pairs claim two Ties that they will develop for the rest of the day. Votes should guide them, but allow freedom to pick a Tie that they have passion to explore. As a facilitator, you may want to combine similar Ties before dividing them up. Direct selections to ensure that all the top Ties are being worked, and that there is little redundancy.

  Next, have them search for images that go with the Ties that they picked. Have a stack of magazines to raid for text and pictures to create simple collages. Magazines have an advantage over Googling in this exercise since it is an unfocused search, so unexpected connections are more likely.

- **Graffiti:**

  Post collages on the wall and ask everyone to place their thoughts on the sheets, using their stream of consciousness… whatever pops into their heads. Spend less than thirty seconds at each collage and build on written thoughts too. Rotating from station to station works best.

  After everyone has contributed to all the collages, have pairs collect their marked-up collages for the next exercise.

- **Big Ideas**

  Ask pairs to generate all five types of Big Ideas for each Tie. Allot at least 30 minutes for each one. Bring worksheets for each type of Big Idea, using the descriptions in Chapter 4 as a guide. The graffiti collages can spark thoughts.

  Let them concentrate on one worksheet at a time. It may be helpful to take time outs to share best ideas. This may stimulate other pairs' thinking, even though they are working on unique Ties.

- **Imagination Boards**

  Pairs should choose their favorite Big Idea candidates for each tie, no more than one or two. Utilize the Imagination Board template to expand on each Big Idea. This is best done on a computer in a targeted search for images. Distribute the template through email, and collect finished boards at the end so you can share with the group.

Big Ideas and Imagination Boards are likely to have some rough edges at the end of the day, so plan to clean them up with a smaller team. Save all the work-product from the Big Idea Session to fill in missing gaps.

APPENDIX 2:
BEACHCOMBING VERBS

accumulate	abate	absorb	accelerate	access
admit	acquire	activate	adapt	add
amend	adsorb	adjust	age	alter
arrest	amplify	analyse	apply	arrange
attack	assemble	assist	associate	attach
bite	attenuate	avert	attract	avoid
boil	balance	beat	ball up	bind
brighten	bleed	blend	bend	blow
catch	boost	bounce	block	break-down
check	broaden	build	break	burst
clear	cancel	capture	burn	carve
cohere	categorize	center	carry	charge
combust	chew	circulate	change	clean
conceal	chop	coalesce	classify	coat
congeal	close	collect	coarsen	combine
contact	collapse	communicate	color	compete
confuse	compare	conduct	compensate	conform
convert	concentrate	constrict	confine	consume
copy	connect	contain	construct	control
cover	contract	cook	contribute	coordinate
curb	convey	corrode	cool	couple
darken	denature	flatten	count	condition
drink	correct	creep	crush	crystalize
deepen	curve	cut	decompress	damage
demolish	decipher	decode	delay	decrease
destroy	defend	deflect	deposit	deliver
diagnose	densify	deplete	deteriorate	desiccate

direct	detect	deter	dig	develop
dispose	declaw	diffuse	disintegrate	dilute
distribute	differentiate	discharge	dissolve	disperse
drain	discern	dissociate	drag	distinguish
electrify	disseminate	divide	dump	draft
empty	divert	dull	elongate	emerge
enhance	dry	eliminate	enclose	energize
eradicate	elevate	emulsify	envelope	equalize
exchange	emulate	entertain	evade	evaporate
export	enter	etch	explode	exploit
fasten	erect	expand	extend	extract
find	exhaust	express	fade	fake
food	expose	facilitate	fill	filter
focus	fabricate	fetch	float	flood
fracture	feed	fix	flush	fly
grade	flex	fluoresce	force	form
guide	fit	follow	frighten	fuse
harden	harm	freeze	get	grab
hear	flow	generate	grow	guard
hold	fold	grip	handle	harden
ignore	free	halt	highlight	heat
invert	grasp	haul	hinder	hit
increase	harmonize	import	identify	isolate
inspect	help	hook	inject	improve
interface	homogenize	impede	integrate	turn
light	imitate	inhibit	introduce	intensify
locate	inform	instruct	lessen	ionize
melt	install	interrupt	link	knock
modulate	interpret	join	lower	lift
move	jam	lengthen	mark	load

narrow	launch	limit	mobilize	lubricate
offset	lighten	loosen	motivate	measure
organize	lock	manipulate	observe	modify
paint	maintain	mix	oppose	mount
permit	merge	monitor	perceive	naturalize
polymerize	moisturize	mutate	plug	magnify
pressurize	multiply	operate	match	oppress
project	neutralize	oxidize	produce	pack
pulse	open	penetrate	protect	permeate
push	orient	plan	purify	polish
read	part	postpone	quantify	preserve
redeploy	persist	process	rate	prohibit
refresh	position	promote	record	pull
relax	prevent	purge	refocus	pursue
renew	proliferate	rank	reinforce	qualify
replicate	pump	recognize	relocate	react
resonate	prioritize	reduce	repel	recover
retrieve	raise	register	reroute	refract
shape	rebuild	release	resume	reject
shine	redirect	repeat	sever	remove
shrink	regenerate	reproduce	shield	replace
sink	relay	restrict	shorten	resemble
slow	repair	reveal	signal	retain
sniff	reposition	shed	slide	shake
reverse	restore	shoot	smooth	shift
rip	return	sign	soil	show
rub	sharpen	slam	sterilize	simulate
scale	ship	smell	rid	slip
scratch	shut	soften	rotate	snap
seize	situate	spay	scent	solubilize

serve	smash	revive	seal	ride
spill	soak up	roll	sense	round
spread	revise	rupture	specify	sand
stand	rock	scatter	shave	score
stimulate	run	screw	spoil	secure
strain	scan	send	stabilize	separate
strip	screen	sort	steer	sequence
sum	select	split	store	speed
survive	set	stab	stretch	spot
sweep	spin	steady	substitute	stamp
synchronize	squeeze	stop	suppress	stick
taper	start	stress	swallow	straighten
terminate	stir	sublimate	swing	strike
thwart	strengthen	supply	tame	suck
torque	stroke	sustain	temper	surround
transfer	supplement	swim	thin	swap
transport	suspend	tear	tighten	switch
widen	swell	thicken	trade	tap
transmute	systematize	tie	transmit	tension
twist	target	trace	turn	thrust
untie	test	translate	Unlock	tighten
wound	thump	trigger	vibrate	tip
wet	toughen	unload	weld	train
vaporize	transform	vary	wrap	weaken
warn	trap	trick	unite	taste
wipe				

APPENDIX 3:
NAKED TRUTH TEMPLATES

Consumer Need:

REAL	DEAL
A Desire A Fact of Life A Habit A Personal Value *And Why*	*But*

Remedy:

UNDERLYING PROBLEM	SOLUTION
The primary issue with today's remedies and what causes it.	*Eliminate it by . . .* *Work around it by . . .* *And How*

Market Force:

DYNAMIC	RESPONSE
What is Rising *What is Falling* *What is Unchanging* *And Why*	*Ride it by . . .* *Counter it by . . .* *And How*

REFERENCES

Joseph Campbell, 1949. *The Hero Has a Thousand Faces*. Pantheon Books.

Abraham H. Maslow, 1943. *A Theory of Human Motivation.* Article in Psychological Review.

James A. Prochaska, John C. Norcross and Carlo C. DiClemente, 1994. *Changing for Good.* William Morrow.

Everette M. Rogers, 1962. *Diffusion of Innovation.* The Free Press, a division of Simon & Schuster, Inc.

Steve Diller, Darrel Rhea and Nathan Shedroff, 2008. *Making Meaning: How Successful Businesses Deliver Meaningful Consumer Experiences.* Peachpit, a division of Pearson Education.

Edward De Bono, 1992. *Serious Creativity: Using the Power of Lateral Thinking to Create New Ideas*. Harper Business.

Chip Heath and Dan Heath, 2007. *Made to Stick.* Random House

Edited by Arthur B. Markman and Kristen L. Wood, 2009. *Tools for Innovation: The Science Behind the Practical Methods that Drive New Ideas.* Oxford University Press.

Tony Buzan, 1996. *The Mind Map Book: How to Use Radiant Thinking to Maximize Your Brain's Untapped Potential.* Penguin Books

www.ingramcontent.com/pod-product-compliance
Lightning Source LLC
Chambersburg PA
CBHW021407170526
45164CB00002B/538